Learning to Love

From Conflict to Communication

Darren Twa

© 2012 Darren Twa

BlackStripesPublishing.com

BlackStripes Publishing
Kenmore, WA

Learning to Love: From Conflict to Communication
ISBN 978-0-9823574-3-9

For my children
that they may love sacrificially

Contents

Understanding Value Systems

Discovering Values

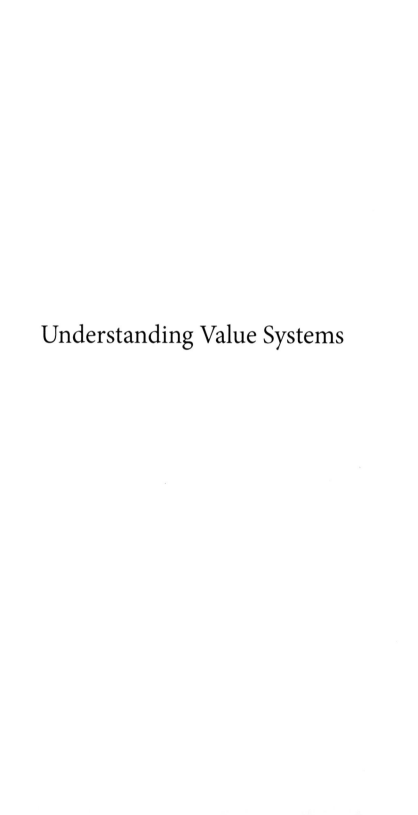

Understanding Value Systems

1 Value Systems

Your value system is the sum total of your ideas and beliefs. Some values come from what you have been taught, while others are based on your positive and negative experiences. Regardless of the source, as you live you form preferences and your own personal perspective on life. Every assessment you make, and opinion you form, merges to create your unique value system.

However, when many people think of values, they often think only of moral beliefs. This is too limited; *values are more than moral beliefs*. Not everything in a person's value system is a matter of right or wrong because some of what we like or dislike is completely non-moral. There is a broad spectrum of human pleasure, and we do not all share equivalent levels of enjoyment for any activity. Our individual preferences for food, hobbies, and entertainment are all examples of non-moral values.

Imagine a bar chart containing millions of bars. Now imagine that each bar represents one of your values, such as honesty or spicy food. Every value you hold is on that chart, whether moral or non-moral. Expand your sense of the complexity of it: imagine bars for every flavor of ice cream; and, the more you like a flavor, the higher the bar. Each value is a preference or opinion about *something* in life, and the height of any bar is a reflection on how important that value is to you. Furthermore, the intensity of your reaction to life circumstances reveals how high each bar is for its related value.

No two people perfectly share the same value system. Yours is unique because no one else could possibly have each and every value at the exact same level as you. This complexity explains why relationships are both so exciting and so difficult at the same time.

The basis of relationship

Relationships are based on common values. You experience this every day as you are drawn to those who share your interests and moral ideas. You also prefer to avoid people who do not share your values, whether morals, manners, or interests. In fact, it is difficult to enjoy a relationship with someone whose values substantially differ from your own.

We often form relationships around non-moral values, such as hobbies and entertainment. However, in order to develop strong relationships with others, we need to hold certain additional values in common since the quality of any relationship is directly linked to how *important* each of the shared values is to the participants. While each person decides which values are most important to him, moral values typically determine the success or failure of a relationship.

For example, two people may share a common interest in football, but if one thinks the other is a liar and a thief, they likely will not develop a deep friendship. On the other hand, if we have a mutual interest in keeping our neighborhood safe, our ability to work together should not be hindered by differing views on athletics.

Relationships grow over time as the participants move together in values. When people first meet, they often know little of what the other values. Each person makes assumptions, some true and some false. Yet, over time, if they discover that they agree on their principal values, the relationship will deepen and grow stronger.

This is also true with regard to all family relationships. Parents usually seek to instill their values into their children. Yet, as a child grows, she forms her own unique value system. She variously retains or rejects her parent's values, and she chooses how much influence each value will have in her own life. The quality of relationship the parent and child share is completely dependent on how much they agree on each other's *most cherished* values.

You live your value system

Of course, the values that we actually hold are the ones we demonstrably live. If we claim to hold a moral value yet act in opposition to it, then a different value undoubtedly motivated our action. For example, if I claim to value truth but occasionally lie, then there is something more important to me than telling the truth. My lies prove that I hold at least one other value more deeply than honesty, even if it only manifests occasionally. We always live by our values, even if every action has many values influencing it.

Every family or organization has rules or expectations of what each member should or should not do. The degree to which we adhere to those expectations reveals how much we agree with them. And, although we might not agree with a rule or expectation, we still might live according to it in order to preserve our relationships. In that case, our choice demonstrates that we value *the relationship* more than we value choosing our own rules or having our own way.

Likewise, in the workplace we may not agree with every requirement imposed on us, but—at the very minimum—we value the paycheck we receive. But once the "level of pay" value dips below one or more other critical values, we will quit that job and seek another. Knowing this, a manager who wishes to retain quality people will seek to understand and, if possible, fulfill the employment values and expectations of his personnel.

Inner conflict

Our *actions* are the primary indicators of the values we hold because the values that we live by are deeply connected to what is most important to us. When you struggle in making an important decision, it is either because you do not yet have a firm value regarding that issue or because you lack the information you need to match it to the values you currently hold. Conversely, strongly held values yield a greater ability to make choices in life.

Consequently, inner conflict arises from an attempt to live with multiple differing values. If values contend within us, we feel frustration while considering which values we should follow; but ultimately, some prevail over others and *our actions reveal our deepest values*. We always live by our values, although every action has many values influencing it.

Some of our values are good, and thus we do what is good. Yet even when we have less than noble desires, we often choose not to express those values because the negative consequences of our actions will affect something significant to us. So, even when we believe that we are not living according to our desires, we always are. For example, a man may want something enough to steal it, yet he does not steal it; his desires to avoid prison and the shame of being caught overrule his desire to possess. Thus, we constantly suppress certain values because we fear the consequences of acting on them.

Although precedence is always given to the values that are most important to us, there is always flux within our value systems. Values producing positive results are reinforced, while negative outcomes cause us to lower a value's importance. Since we measure values based on the consequences they *seem* to produce, we often draw erroneous conclusions about them. Therefore, our selection of values should be guided by what is *good for relationship*, thereby producing actions that enhance relationship.

To be completely at peace within yourself, there must be conformity between your *preferred* values and how you live. You experience inner conflict when you must choose among several weakly held values rather than from firmly held beliefs. Such conflict is resolved by determining which values will be most important to you, along with the willful choice to live according to them. In order to improve your relationships, you need a firm commitment to a value system that builds strong relationships.

Recap:

- Who you are is defined by what you value.
- You live your most deeply held values.
- Relational enjoyment flows from shared values.

Think:

- What are my most cherished values?
- What impact do they have on my relationships?
- Do they enhance or hinder my relationships?

2 Conflict

When you experience a disagreement with someone, it is always a disagreement over one of your values. That is, you see the matter one way, and the other person sees it another way. It may be something trivial or something extremely important to you, but *all conflict in relationship is conflict over value system.*

Agreement draws us closer together, whereas disagreement drives people apart. The more important something is to you—the more you value it—the greater the conflict you will have when someone disagrees with you or obstructs your plans. This conflict over value system is the destructive factor in *all* relationships.

For example, when someone first feels "in love," one portion of her emotion flows from her beliefs about the *other* person's value system. She tends to believe the other person holds values similar to hers. However, as the relationship progresses, she begins to realize that they do not share all the values she first anticipated. During times of disappointment and conflict, she discovers the other person's real values; and, as the illusion of common values breaks down, so too do some of her positive emotions.

Every quarrel or fight is a battle over whose values will prevail. It may be as trivial as deciding which movie to watch, or as severe as quitting your job because your boss mistreats you. As long as you both agree, you do not have conflict because you are living a *shared* value system. But each time you disagree, the level of conflict is directly proportional to the importance each of you places on the conflicting value. The more our value systems differ from each other, the more our relationships will suffer.

Each value we hold has the potential to cause division in relationship. Since differing values produce conflict that results in negative emotions and damaged relationships, we must ask, "Is having what I value more important to me than any relationships affected by my choice?" When we do choose to live by values not agreeable to others, we prioritize that freedom over relationship. When we choose different values from our wife, husband, parent, or child, we are making a choice between values and relationship. Deliberately choosing values that are significantly different from another is a choice to limit portions of relationship with that person.

Prolonging conflict in relationship demonstrates that what you value is more important to you than the relationship. You would rather have your own way than have the relationship progress and improve; and, if you cannot have your own way, then you are willing to let the relationship degrade. People argue because they hold values different from each other; and, unless they view the relationship as more important than the matter producing conflict, they will be more willing to dissolve the relationship than resolve their differences in value system.

For example, couples often disagree about how money should be earned, spent, or saved. Each idea flows from inner values, and one person may want the pleasure of spending it and the other the security of saving it. Therefore, when a couple disagrees about money, they need to be able to understand and express the *values* driving their desires and feelings. If they cannot come to an agreement on values, they need to at least agree that their relationship is more important to them than their choice of how to spend money. Hopefully, from the greater value they place on relationship will come the means by which to resolve conflicts over any lesser values of finance.

Happiness in relationship

If we truly desire to have good relationships, we need to resolve conflicts by changing values. The values that need to change may belong to you, the other person, or even both of you. We will not agree on the importance of everything in life, but to grow closer we must agree on the values we deem *most* significant.

Good relationships are formed only by sharing your true values. To be accepted and liked for values that you only pretend to possess is not real relationship, and it will never bring deep fulfillment. If values you hold are interfering with your relationships, you need to choose whether you would rather improve your relationships or keep your current values.

Lying is destructive to relationship because liars only pretend to share a common value system with you. They want the *benefits* of relationship without truly sharing the values that *produce* relationship. People often lie in order to prevent conflict, but they only produce more conflict once their dishonesty and hypocrisy are discovered.

Happiness comes from freely expressing who we are (the full revelation of our deepest values), being open and honest about what we desire, and yet still finding acceptance. However, we often fail to achieve happiness in relationship because conflict produces fear that we will be rejected *because of* what we value. We then hide our true desires from others, leaving us lonely in the midst of relationship. However, if we cannot share the deepest values of our hearts and still be accepted, then the relationship will never bring us the fulfillment we desire. We will continue to have conflict with each other because, without openness, we will not understand the values that are really producing conflict. Resolving conflict requires accepting others rather than simply criticizing them because, even when we know we need improvement, we crave acceptance while we change our lives to match our highest virtues.

Recap:

- Conflict flows from disagreement on what is most valuable to you.
- Relationships suffer when you value something more than the relationship.
- Relational conflict must be resolved by changing values.
- Openness is required to discuss values.

Think:

- Which values are producing my current conflicts?

3 Desires

Before you can resolve conflicts in your life, you must first understand how your value system is ordered. All of your values—from the least to the greatest—are expressed through only three areas of desire. Your unique set of values determines what you do and do not want to happen but is conveyed through aspects of life common to us all: physical appetites, how we want people to perceive us, and through personal domain.

Appetites

You have many desires simply because you must care for your body. These include food, air, and shelter. You also have the need to be touched and held in positive, loving ways, and to have your sexual desires fulfilled. All share these basic desires, but the importance of each varies from person to person according to his own value system. Our choices in life are influenced by our values, but expressed through our appetites.

There is nothing wrong with eating or satisfying any of the body's natural appetites and desires for pleasure. But, in order to have good relationships, it is better to consider the values of others rather than only seeking to satisfy one's own appetites. Even though our natural desires are all good, the emotions associated with them can tempt us to pursue a pleasurable response even when our actions are relationally damaging.

The value we place on a pleasurable appetite can be measured by how its loss or denial affects us. We often have strong emotional reactions when anything interferes with the pleasures we seek. If we become angry when required to cease an activity we wish to continue, or if we refuse to relinquish something an authority in our life has prohibited, it shows how strongly we value it.

Bodily appetites that produce pleasure often become sources of addiction to gratification thereby reinforcing a selfish value system. The danger in being driven by pleasure is that it results in an unwillingness to change negative values. If our practice of any appetite is so excessive that it harms others, or if we engage in foolish risks to fulfill it, our relationships will suffer. Additionally, it is difficult to act in ways that benefit others once pleasing ourselves becomes an ingrained habit.

Reputation

We are also highly motivated by the desire to have others like and approve of us. How much we seek approval in a relationship is directly proportional to the importance we place on that relationship. In our desperate desire for acceptance, we freely modify many of our values, thus conforming to the values held by the group with which we seek association. Furthermore, it is not uncommon for people to act or speak insincerely in order to enhance their reputations and gain status.

People also tend to avoid provoking rejection. Experiencing painful consequences for non-conformity during one's youth may result in an adult who feels anxiety should he differ from others during social encounters. Thus, we willingly "play our part" believing that revealing our differing values will result in a negative outcome toward us, whether at home, in the workplace, or in any other social group. Whenever we speak or act in order to placate others, or to have them like or adore us, we demonstrate that the relationship is more important to us than the values we disguise. If our desire to be accepted becomes strong enough to compel us to act against the values that we hold, we experience inner conflict.

Peer pressure derives from a desire for approval, whether through appearance, behavior, or language. For example, a child who wants his friends to accept him may do something he believes is wrong in order to become part of the group. He feels inner turmoil because he is attempting to live by two conflicting value systems: his parents' and his friends'. Ultimately, the values *and relationships* that he considers most important will prevail.

Having people like us often shapes how we dress and present ourselves. A woman who deems it highly important to appear beautiful in the eyes of others will expend money and energy in achieving that goal. It is not wrong to look attractive, but it is important to understand the values within that make it such a crucial issue. Acceptance based predominantly on physical appearance can never produce lasting relationship because it ignores the more important aspects of personhood.

People often hide their true values because they are afraid of losing status by being open about them. They want people *to believe* they are good, even when they know in their hearts that they are not. In other words, we often want others to think we have one value system when, in fact, we hold another. Meanwhile, we condemn as hypocrites those who seek to gain prestige for that which does not conform to inner reality.

Therefore, we must never manipulate a situation for personal recognition. If we specifically act to gain the approval of others we cannot be truly honoring them. We are improperly focused on that which helps ourselves rather than on that which benefits others. When we fear rejection, our lives become tainted with a deep love of self that seeks the admiration of others rather than a willingness to love them.

It is not wrong to want people to approve of you. However, rather than making choices based solely on what others think, you need to choose the best values for relationship. Although it may seem counterintuitive, it is better to face rejection for the values you hold rather than be accepted for ones you pretend to hold. Nevertheless, if your values are destroying your relationships, you need to carefully evaluate them.

Domain

Domain may be about wealth, possessions, or simply having our own will be done. It is a desire to have what we want, when we want it. It encompasses most of what people spend their efforts in life pursuing; and, although it can enhance our relationships, it can never replace our need for them.

People love power. They value control and will manipulate or exploit others in order to keep it. Having power and authority over others is not the problem; using it to have people serve you instead of using it to also benefit them is the problem. Yet love of power is not limited only to those with great power or authority. It also appears as rebellion against authority, expressed by lack of submission or by attempting to manipulate those in authority.

Relationships suffer when there is an unequal division of power and those with more power do not seek the good of those under their authority. We reveal our love of power every time we demand that our families serve us rather than finding joy in serving them. The manager who treats his employees badly may gain temporary results, but he loses the extensive long-term benefits of a workforce that respects him.

When a couple has different ideas of how money should be spent it often relates to issues of security or fairness. They will argue over who spends more pleasing oneself, or they may feel cheated if they do not get to purchase what they prefer. This same type of conflict also happens in business and in government, because we all want to have wealth used to achieve our own plans.

Deep inside the person who loves power reside fear and selfishness. He might be able to hide these from others; however, he is not able to hide his lack of love. The depth of peoples' desire for money is revealed by what they will do, compromise, or lose in order to achieve great wealth. But true greatness is demonstrated by honoring and loving others, not in the supposed security and happiness that wealth provides. Those who hoard money, steal, and exploit others for financial gain destroy the relationships associated with those they harm.

There is nothing wrong with enhancing your own domain. But when it comes at the expense of your family and business relationships, you need to evaluate the true value of relational happiness. This cannot be bought; it comes only through living relationally enhancing values.

Desires and relationship

The three areas of desire are natural and there is nothing wrong with them; however, our *expressions* of them can either enhance or destroy our relationships. Since all of our values and desires affect relationship, and since our greatest happiness comes from good relationships, we should seeks values that enhance rather than hinder relationship. The following examples demonstrate the connection between values, desires and relationship.

We all share a common bodily appetite for food, but for some it becomes an issue of overeating. I value eating reasonable portions of healthy food, but I also value gorging myself on tasty cuisine. Often these two values conflict. My true value is the one that I live. If I live according to the second value, I will gain weight and my relationships will suffer. I will be concerned about what my spouse and others think about me, and I may not have the energy to play with my children.

We also all share a physical and emotional need for touching and being touched. However, if I do not limit whom I touch and how I touch them, there will be profound relational consequences for my actions. Without strong values limiting my desires, my relationships will suffer or be destroyed.

Everyone desires positive recognition from others,

yet many children seek acceptance from their peers by doing activities of which they know their parents disapprove. We cannot please everyone, so while attempting to gain the approval of some, we often alienate others. Our deepest values determine whose attention we seek and which relationships we will sacrifice in order to gain respect in another.

We tend to think that our own ideas are better than the ideas of others, so we often want people to submit to our will. However, in pressing for control, I can cause people to dislike my attitude, if not me personally. Whenever I demand my own way, I damage the relationships with those I seek to control.

People driven to gain great wealth and possessions often do so at the expense of others. If we exploit others to become rich, we gain a reputation that will haunt all of our relationships. If I spend my family's income to purchase toys for myself without regard for the needs of my spouse or children, they will resent my selfishness.

Your value system determines how you evaluate each part of your life. If you value pleasure over reputation, you will act for pleasure regardless of what people think of you. If you value money over reputation, you will act to gain wealth even if it gives others a negative perception of you. If you value power more than you love others, it will be demonstrated by your exploiting, manipulating, and controlling people rather than helping them.

All three areas of desire affect relationship. The values we hold either make our relationships stronger or tear them apart. Unless we evaluate the positive and negative outcomes of each one, we will fail to resolve conflicts.

If I choose to express desires in a way that destroys my relationships, it reveals how much I value myself more than others. But if I wish to pursue quality relationships, I must share the same positive values held by those I love.

Desires can work for us or against us. Pleasure, approval, wealth, and power should be used for building healthy, loving relationships. Our values determine if our pursuit of them will be detrimental to others, or if they will enhance relationship. Values that honor others are inherently relationship building. But unbridled pursuit of pleasure, approval, power, and money diminishes our ability to have, pursue, maintain, and enjoy relationships. In contrast, when two people seek to honor and love each other, they become driven more by values than by desires. Their relationship will be meaningful, beautiful and desirable—resulting in lasting joy; and, ultimately, their desires will be fulfilled in ways that please them both.

All of your values can influence your relationships, and you express them through common means. Your desires for physical pleasure, the approval of others, and to be in control are natural. Together, they represent every desire you face, and they reveal the underlying values that affect your relationships with others. Being adept in understanding these three areas of desire will help you understand your emotions and, more significantly, give you deep insight into your values.

Recap:

- Your values are expressed through three areas of desire.
- Appetites are usually issues of bodily needs and pleasures.
- Reputation is the desire to be respected or adored.
- Domain is desire for power, wealth, and control.

Think:

- Which of the three areas of desire dominate my relationships?
- Are my relationships being enhanced or hindered by my current expression of these desires?

4 Emotions

Emotions are like the lights on the dashboard of a car. They provide information about something happening elsewhere. If we treat the indicator light as the problem by smashing it or covering it up, we do not address the real issue. It may relieve us to not see the warning light on, but we will eventually suffer for ignoring its message and the designated problem. People who seek only to *control* their emotions do not deal with the underlying reasons for having those emotions. They are determined to make the light on the dashboard change apart from addressing issues with the internal workings of the car.

In order to improve our relationships we need to focus on changing our value systems. However, sometimes the values producing conflict can be difficult to identify. Fortunately, emotions can be used to gain insight into which values we deem most important and which ones need to change.

Emotions reveal values

There is a simple connection between emotions, desires, and values. First, our value systems determine what we want life to be like. Then, we express those values through the three areas of desire (appetites, reputation, and domain) acting to bring good into our lives and avoiding what we believe will harm us. Finally, *our emotions reveal whether or not our value systems are being fulfilled or denied.* They are a response to whether or not we have received what we desire.

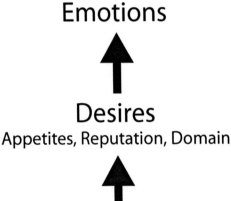

Emotions

Desires
Appetites, Reputation, Domain

Values

When our values are fulfilled we usually feel happy. Experiencing emotions that you enjoy indicates that you are obtaining what you value. Getting what you want or having life your way results in satisfaction and pleasure. In this way, *emotions reveal your values.* The stronger the emotional response, the more important the underlying value being fulfilled is to you.

When we do not achieve our desires and goals we

feel miserable and upset. Experiencing emotions that you do not enjoy indicates that your values are not being fulfilled. You feel negative emotion when you do not get what you want and are not having life lived your way. When people or situations do not meet your expectations, whether in relationships at home or because of difficulties at work, your values are revealed through your emotions. The stronger you sense these negative feelings, the more significant the underlying values are to you.

If we fail to recognize that our value systems determine the expression of our desires and are the ultimate source of our emotions, we will be unable to resolve emotional issues and their relational effects. Many people attempt to cease being angry without understanding and dealing with its source: *value conflict* between them and another person. Until the real issue is dealt with, feelings of anger will not be subdued.

Even when damaging values are not revealed to us by our desires, our emotions can be useful in determining the values we need to change. Values that harm relationships always manifest as selfish desires and often lead to emotions that destroy relationships. Emotions are the voice of the heart—you need to listen to them. When your values shout, they do so through strong emotions. But even when speaking softly, they still reveal what is truly important to you.

Emotions and Relationship

Although any fulfillment of our values can feel good, our greatest happiness comes from experiencing positive emotions in the context of relationship. Relationships that make us happy are based on values we consider enjoyable, satisfying, and fulfilling. Thus, if we wish to experience the joy we desire in relationship, we must understand emotions and the effect they have on relationship. We must know what *causes* us to become angry, sad, or frustrated so that we might be transformed into people who experience enjoyable relationships.

Emotions themselves can also benefit and enhance our relationships. To make this happen, we must focus our attention on using emotions to strengthen relationship. For example, people do not like to associate with those who produce negative feelings in them. We prefer people who make us happy to those who generate fear, anger, or sadness. Even as children, we quickly learn to associate our emotions with the people who cause them. We gravitate toward people who make us feel good and avoid those who make us feel bad. Emotions are powerful forces in establishing, maintaining—and damaging—relationships.

Therefore, we need to consider our actions in terms of relationship and how our values affect those around us. If I consistently produce negative emotions in others, then something about me needs to change; otherwise people will avoid me. Unless I change the reasons for my words and actions, I will fail to create and maintain meaningful relationships. However, if people feel good around me, they will gravitate toward me. They will enjoy my presence and want to develop relationships with me. Having this effect on people should never be done to manipulate: it should be the natural outcome of genuinely honoring and loving others.

Emotions themselves do not teach us what is right or wrong morally or what is good for relationship: they only reveal fulfillment of values. Furthermore, quality of relationship should only be evaluated over the long term because one instant of positive or negative emotion is not a trustworthy measure of a relationship's health. Finally, the more important the value and the stronger the desire, the more powerfully we feel an emotion. That is why strong negative emotions reveal values that must always be addressed in order to protect a relationship.

Recap:

- Emotions are a natural response to fulfilled or thwarted desires.

- The stronger the emotion, the more important the value driving it is to you.

- Emotions are not a moral guide; they are window into your value system.

Think:

- What are the values driving my significant emotional reactions?

5   Resolving Conflict

Since all conflict in relationship is conflict over value system, the only way to remove conflict is by agreeing on values. Not all conflict over value system is relationally destructive. Usually only moral issues and excessive indulgence in non-moral desires have a negative impact on relationship. But where the conflicting values are hindering or damaging a relationship, only a change of values can restore and improve the relationship. Until one or both people change and agree to live by a common value system there will continue to be conflict.

We all know that forgiveness plays a part in removing the consequences for our actions. Unfortunately, while many models of forgiveness seek closure, they do not promote relationship because they neglect to address the underlying issues of value system. Since resolving conflict requires *agreement* on values, a correct method must stimulate *changing* values. The value producing the conflict must be altered, and there must be agreement on how each person should now act toward the other. Furthermore, problems created by the previous value system must not be allowed to hinder the progressing relationship.

There are four steps in resolving conflict and repairing damaged relationships. Both parties involved in the conflict must participate *willingly* because the steps are shared between the people involved. The four steps are like the wheels on a car: you cannot experience a smooth ride without all four in place.

Step 1: Admit fault

People need to admit when they are wrong. Unless at least one person is willing to admit that he made a mistake or was acting in a way that was damaging to the relationship, there will be no progress in improving it. Without *verbal* acknowledgement that an action was wrong, there will be an ongoing obstruction in the relationship.

Admitting fault is a declaration that the relationship cannot be built around a conflict-producing value. It is the first step in coming to an agreement on value system because it is an acknowledgement that my particular value was wrong and yours was right. When I admit my fault, I am admitting *my* value caused the problem and that *my* value needs to change in order to resolve the problem.

It is not enough to realize that what I did was wrong, even if I seek to change how I live. If I do not express it to the person I mistreated, our relationship accumulates emotional pain that is not removed. Only by admitting fault can I bring relief and positive emotion to the one I hurt.

Although it is humbling to admit we were wrong,

we gain greater strength to change from it. Humility makes changing our values easier, and changing our values is the prerequisite to building better relationships. Thus, the first step in our becoming free of selfish values is expressing them as trouble causing agents. We gain strength to change because we no longer hide our old values and because we admit that our previous value system failed us, requiring the need for new values.

Of course, humility requires that we trust another person to respond as one who has also made his share of mistakes. Humility that encounters a harsh response often finds an excuse to avoid change. The relationship then enters a death-spiral of resentment as both parties begin unconstructively criticizing one another's faults.

Step 2: Replace values

After verbalizing the problem, we need to *change the value that produced the conflict*. When we replace a value that has been harming a relationship, we also need to change the way we act so that we do not continue hurting the other person. Without change, the problem will re-emerge because the difference in value system has not been resolved. Only an agreement on values brings two people together and prepares them for a future without continuing conflict—at least in this area.

The only way to permanently break bad habits is to replace them with good ones. In order to stop an action or thought pattern, you need to create or develop intersecting values that have a greater importance to you than the bad habits you wish to cease. Until your new values have more priority than your old ones, you will continue to live the old values. Admitting fault without replacing values provides only temporary improvement to the relationship. To achieve long-term results, values must change because the sincerity of our words is always demonstrated through permanent transformation in how we live.

Living by a new value in the area that previously produced conflict is a living admission that the value and the relational damage it produced were interconnected. By seeing the action that led to the reaction (that is, the value that led to the conflict), you can better understand the nature of relationships and the need to adopt better values. These new values bring hope to both people that the relationship will be better than it was before.

Step 3: Forgive

Once the person whose actions produced the conflict has pledged change, the injured person needs to forgive. Forgiveness is a promise you make to the one who has hurt you that you will not punish him *relationally* for what he has done. With forgiveness, the relationship receives a new starting point subsequent to the conflict. Because the person's value that produced the conflict has now changed, the forgiver must not treat the person according to his *previous* value system but according to his *new* one. In a sense, the old person is gone and a new and better person is there.

Removing the relational consequences of an offence may require that a person still be held accountable in other ways for his actions. It is inappropriate for a person to expect that forgiveness immediately exempts him from certain punishments or restitutions required for causing harm to another person. Taking responsibility for what one has done is a strong indicator that a person will truly replace the value that created the problem. Seeking forgiveness is always about the desire to have a relationship restored; it is never merely a means to avoid punishment for what one has done.

In order to truly forgive someone, you must not seek to get even with him before he asks for forgiveness. By taking revenge on someone, you make true forgiveness impossible because you have already made that person pay for his actions. Revenge contributes to the destruction of a relationship and attests that you have values that need to change. Any harm you bring against another person *before or after he asks forgiveness* will require you to address your own wrong values.

Forgiveness is not an issue of how we feel since it operates independently from our emotions: it is an act of the will. However, once a person genuinely promises change, the one who was harmed will have an easier time recovering emotionally from any grievance. Until the feelings of hurt diminish, the forgiver needs to act according to a value that expresses his joy that the other person has changed. When we forgive, we must not recall memories of an offense in order to harm or punish the other person.

It may be necessary to discuss the issue with the other person so that he understands how his actions have damaged the relationship. When endeavoring to produce change in the other person, focus on expressing your underlying values and attempt to understand his. In order to more quickly come to the point of conflict, do not assume you know what he values, and do not focus on your emotions and desires. This will help prevent him from feeling attacked or rejected, prompting better discussion and less resistance.

Your feeling offended by someone does not mean that he was truly at fault, or that he even knows he has done something wrong. Until you begin discussing the issue, the conflict in the relationship may be completely unknown to the other person. When you do make it known, give the person time to consider what you are saying about the problem without demanding immediate action.

Please note that forgiveness is not merely pretending that no offense happened. Rather, forgiveness is an act of the will toward someone who is *demonstrably endeavoring* to change his value system. Attempting to "forgive" someone who refuses to acknowledge the problem in the relationship only contributes to the demise of the relationship because it does not require a change of values. True forgiveness wipes the slate clean of the relational damage only because it trusts that there will be no further relational damage since the value causing the conflict has changed.

Step 4: Reconcile

The last step in resolving conflict is restoration of the relationship. Even when people have changed and forgiven, it is sometimes difficult to continue the relationship either because of embarrassment, issues of trust, or a history of painful experiences. Whatever the reason, people often prefer to turn away from one another rather than work to improve relationships. This is unfortunate because, after resolving the conflicting value, the two are now positioned to experience a better relationship than ever before.

Reconciliation between two people who had previously experienced conflict is the surest sign that they understand how important their relationship is. Instead of dwelling on the past painful conflict, they recognize that a closer relationship can now form because *they now have more agreement on their values than ever before.* All relationships are based on common values, and one of the deepest values two people need to share is the importance of pursuing relationship even beyond the difficult times.

If this process of resolving conflict does not make the relationship stronger, then some portion of it has been left undone: one of the steps has been avoided. Even as you would not like to drive your car if it were missing one of its wheels, so also each one of these four steps is necessary for the relational restoration process to be intact. Both people must be involved and committed to the relationship. They cannot quit out of embarrassment, resentment, or fear. If the relationship diminishes it is ultimately because someone still does not share the common value of how important *this* relationship is.

Let me illustrate this process with a story. Imagine I am in the habit of leaving a mess in the kitchen and I expect my wife to clean up after me. Of course, she finds this frustrating and, since she has asked me numerous times not to do it, it is negatively impacting our relationship.

It is not enough for me to simply stop leaving a mess. Instead, I first need to acknowledge that my behavior has been wrong and selfish; doing so alleviates much of the tension my wife is feeling toward me. I then need to ask her to forgive me for reducing her to the role of my maid. The reality is that I had not valued her as I ought to have. I have not regarded her as my equal, and selfishly exercised power over her.

If I am sincere, I will now change my value system from one that permits me to leave messes for others to address, to one that cleans up after myself. However, if I do not change, then my words were merely a ruse to avoid conflict. I may even fool myself into thinking I really meant them, but how I *live* proves the real values I hold. Admitting fault without changing only artificially removes the conflict and results in *greater* damage later.

Once I have confessed my fault and asked forgiveness, my wife can now tell by my words that *I recognize* the values that were producing the problem. Furthermore, my promise to work at changing them encourages her to forgive me and not to treat me according to how my old values deserved. Rather, she will treat me as though I have always picked up after myself!

My response to this beautiful gift she has given me is to thank her and do my best not to fail her. Our relationship is better not only because I have changed a selfish value but also because she has forgiven me and will not retaliate for my previous actions.

It is always difficult and painful for people to move together in value system. One or both of them must admit that he has been living selfishly. Relationships often break down during conflict because people are *unwilling to admit selfishness* even though they may be willing to change it. Restoration of relationship requires admitting fault and receiving forgiveness, not merely altering actions. It is not enough to change; one must change with an acknowledgement that the previous behavior was wrong.

A long-term relationship that has gone through struggles of change and openness can produce two people who have deep commitment and love for one another. They grow together in values and become people who act for the benefit of others and not merely for self. People whose relationships fall apart over conflicts never experience the deep joy found in the freedom and openness of sharing values, dreams, and desires; instead, they remain locked in their selfish ways.

Recap:

- Conflict is removed by agreement on values.
- The person who created the conflict must admit his fault, and replace the offending value.
- The person harmed responds by forgiving.
- Forgiveness is offered only to people who recognize and seek to change the values that caused the problem.
- Both people must seek to live in the newly restored relationship.

Think:

- What shortcuts do I take in conflict resolution?
- Are my conflicts resolved in ways that preserve my relationships?

6 Relational Values

My values are a choice of what *I think* is good and best. But when I focus only on picking what is good for me, I will not always pick what is good for those around me. Relationships immediately begin to suffer when participants choose values that serve only themselves rather than others. Although greatest happiness is found in relationship, we foolishly pursue pleasure in momentary desires. We wrongly believe that happiness is bound up in having our selfish expectations fulfilled; but, in reality, it comes from good relationships.

Interpersonal conflict is a result of failing to achieve our own values and desires. Selfish values produce anger and fighting, ultimately destroying relationships. Remember, all conflict in relationship is conflict over value system: We experience some degree of loss every time we fight with one another, but we grow closer when we agree on values.

Although conflict in relationship can be removed

through agreement on values, something more is required. Not only must we agree on common values, we must also choose to live by a value system that contributes positively to relationship. The good news is that one exists. The value system that produces the strongest relationships is based on beneficial love for others.

Beneficial love

By seeking to serve those I love, my relationships gain a focus on how I am connected to others rather than only on how I might fulfill my individual desires. The whole concept of relationship revolves around joining people together rather than separating them. So, instead of focusing on what I want, I must consider the needs of the other person.

Beneficial love demands a willingness to relinquish some of my own desires in order to fulfill the desires of another person. If I truly love someone and want her to know and feel it, I need to do what she values. In return, as she acts to fulfill my values, I also feel loved. Instead of seeking happiness regardless of the effect on the other person, I discover a two-fold happiness. First, I experience the happiness of having another person loving me. Second, I experience an additional joy by making another person happy.

Love that benefits others is the best value system for producing and sustaining relationship because it has conflict reduction and resolution built-in. If two people are both trying to please each other rather than only pleasing self, it removes conflict. Desires that we attempt to fulfill selfishly in spite of their effect on the other person are eliminated. If I consider the effects my words and actions will have, I will be careful not to inflict pain or injury on anyone else. Rather than harming others, I will say and do that which makes their lives better.

Beneficial love cannot be artificial. You cannot merely "give in" to the desire of the other person. It must be the true value of your heart to serve or help. Your desire to please the other and build the relationship *must be greater* than your desire to always have your own way. If it is merely an act, you will become frustrated when you are not served the ways you desire. Beneficial love done only for what you will receive in return is not beneficial to the other at all—it is manipulative. That is why beneficial love only works when all participants are seeking this same amazing value system.

Love that benefits others must become the foundation of your value system. It does not necessarily eliminate your other interests or desires, unless they are selfish and contrary to love. But, when used as your most basic moral guide, it can govern your other values and desires. Instead of confusion regarding what you should or should not do, you only need to consider whether or not your actions and desires agree or conflict with beneficial love. If what you desire conflicts with beneficial love, you can be certain that it will also negatively affect your relationships.

For example, let us consider actions that many people consider to be wrong. Murder, lying, and stealing are wrong because they do not benefit the other person. Taken to the extreme, if everyone practiced them, society would break down. Relationships should not be governed by what you *cannot* do in them, but by what you *should be* doing in them. Therefore, instead of a list of negative rules, we can be guided by one positive value. Beneficial love promotes doing good to others, and not merely avoiding doing them harm. Anything that harms our relationships likely flows from some value that is opposed to beneficial love.

You can have the perfect ability to evaluate all aspects of relationship with one simple tool. However, you must be vigilant in examining your values and desires to see if they correspond with beneficial love. If they do—and if your partner in relationship is also being motivated by beneficial love—then your relationship will flourish.

A mutually beneficial relationship

This kind of relationship requires commitment from *both* parties to beneficially love the other. Without dual commitment, the beneficial lover will be exploited. Exploitation always destroys relationship, whereas beneficial love enhances it. Although you can act to benefit those who do not love you in return, wisdom requires that you protect yourself from those who deliberately seek to take advantage of your goodness to them. Allowing someone to exploit you is not love; it is establishing him in a selfish, relationally destructive value system.

Exploitation is the opposite of beneficial love. If we seek to fulfill our desires by using other people, we will hurt them and destroy our relationships. Whenever we force or manipulate others into serving us, we are exploiting them. When people cannot use physical force, they often use anger, threats, sulking, crying, bribes, gifts, and insincere affection or the withholding of it as weapons to manipulate. Any attempt to exploit another will damage that relationship for both the long and short-term.

Therefore, it is crucially important that both people in a relationship be committed to beneficially loving and forgiving each other when they are offended. Holding a grudge damages a relationship as much as selfishness. Beneficial love is tied to forgiveness in that it wills *not to punish* another person for what he has done. Instead of revenge, it prefers restoring relationship and having the other person change his values.

Beneficial love is also tied to personal change. When I love someone, and know that my selfish values cause pain or obstruct our relationship, I will relinquish my own desires in order to benefit the other person. Beneficial love, therefore, drives both the person who needs to change *and* the forgiver who has been offended.

Relationships characterized by love and honor will necessarily have less conflict than those based on selfishness. Truly loving others involves seeking their good and never exploiting them. Good values produce good relationships, and selfish values produce broken relationships and conflict. The reason for this is simple: If two people both have value systems that serve self first, they will experience chronic conflict since neither is focused on doing good for the other.

We all make the mistake of thinking that freedom in choosing our own values will result in happiness and fulfillment. However, the manner in which we live affects not only ourselves but also those around us, ultimately impacting our happiness in relationship. The bottom line is that deciding right and wrong for one's self does not always bring fulfillment, because there are often many unexpected consequences to our choices. Right and wrong need to be evaluated in terms of relationship. The effects our actions have on others cannot be separated from the outcomes they produce in the relationship. Thus, success in relationship is dependent entirely on the value system that underlies our relational values.

Beneficial love at home

We expect the closest and most fulfilling relationships to occur within the family. For this reason, beneficial love naturally emphasizes *sacrifice for others* within the home. Sacrificial love is willing to give and serve even when it costs the lover something. Since family relationships entail commitment, we must invest more in them.

Sacrificial love in the home takes beneficial love to the next level because you are not merely seeking to do good to others, you are also occasionally required to relinquish your own desires in order to grant others theirs. If you are unwilling to give up your own desires in order to fulfill the desires of those you love, then sacrificial love is not one of your deeply held values. Since the strongest familial ties are formed through the mutual surrendering of desires for the sake of others, each member of a household must participate in sacrificial love.

Additionally, the decision to forgive others when they fail to love and honor you is vital to developing a healthy family. Forgiveness is a form of sacrificial love in which the forgiver suffers the loss of his rights for the benefit of the relationship. Even as no one can make you love another person, neither can anyone force you forgive. Both love and forgiveness are choices made to preserve relationship.

Without deliberate effort by all members of a family to love and honor one another, both moral and non-moral values will bring division. Sacrificial love requires the willingness of every participant. To receive the full relational benefits of it, we must practice it in an environment with others who also embrace it.

The worst kind of pain in life is relational pain; but,

by living according to sacrificial love, we can undo the damage caused by selfishness. If we want success in our closest relationships, we must love others by considering their needs before our own and by forgiving them when they hurt us. If we want to have our relationships improve, we must submit our own desires for pleasure, adoration, and control to the moral value of sacrificial love.

Beneficial love in the workplace

Just as every home has values it lives by, every workplace and business has its own value system. Conflict arises at work when the values of the business, managers, and employees differ. In order to improve work relationships, apply the same principles of relationship and value system.

Beneficial love in the workplace primarily takes the form of *honor*. However, when employees genuinely experience beneficial love from an employer, the entire work environment improves. The company that promotes these values in the workplace will reap the benefits of positive relationships and loyal employees.

At minimum, there should be mutual honor. The employee should speak and act toward others in ways that demonstrate a respect for each individual. Employers and managers should speak and act toward employees with the same respect and honor that they expect to receive in return.

Employers need to understand what their employees value. Furthermore, they need to actively seek to meet those values and desires. Employees value job security, a safe and comfortable work environment, equitable wages, and reasonable expectations of their time.

When those needs are met, there is an understanding of honor and commitment to the employees' well being.

The employee should agree with the direction of the business and do all that he can to ensure its success. If you work for someone, you need to be aware that they value having their business be successful, so they do not want you undermining it. You are expected to contribute to the best of your ability.

A business that seeks the benefit of its employees rather than exploits them will find it easier to retain valuable people. The reputation of the company and its management will also improve. Both of these are assets that are not easily recovered once a company squanders them.

Conflicting values between managers, between management and employees, and between employees themselves results in an unproductive and unpleasant work environment. As values align, everyone gains in honor, respect, and contributes to the success of the business.

Universal solution

The greatest source of happiness we can have in life is relational. Although we can find pleasure in appetites and in personal domain, they cannot bring the fulfillment that being truly loved does. Therefore, it makes sense to pursue beneficial love in our relationships so that we, along with those we love, can find deepest personal fulfillment.

The concepts in this book are not difficult to understand; however, changing our values can be very difficult because we like our chosen desires and values, even though we do not always like the results of them. We also prefer to have other people change their values to match ours rather than change our own.

Sometimes it can be extremely difficult to love and honor others. But you must understand that you cannot merely stop doing selfish acts without replacing them with loving ones. Since we have habits and desires that can only change as we continuously practice these new values, it helps to be part of a community of people who are all committed to these same values. Beneficial love can become the value system of your family and govern interactions with your friends.

Beneficial love is the value that can fix all of mankind's relational problems because it prevents selfishness, greed, vengeance, and dishonesty. If all human relationships and interactions were based on beneficial love for others there would be no more war or exploitation. People would care for the environment and seek to help raise those in need out of their poverty. Beneficial love is commitment to a goal bigger than you and your relationships. It is the value system that can make the world a better place, beginning with you, your family, and your friends.

Recap:

- The underlying values in a relationship affect the quality of that relationship.
- Beneficial love prevents exploitation and enhances relationship.
- Sacrificial love is demonstrated by giving up one's own desires to fulfill the desires of another.
- Workplace conflict is an issue of differing value systems.

Think:

- What family conflicts would be reduced if we lived by beneficial love?
- What changes would beneficial love produce in my work environment?
- Which of my values are in conflict with beneficial love?

7 Communication

Truly knowing someone requires that you understand what is most important to her, because a person's value system shapes her character and affects all of her decisions. Furthermore, it is easiest to fulfill a person's values and desires if you first understand them. With a minimal or false idea of what someone values, you will be unable to demonstrate love for her in ways that make her feel loved.

For a relationship to deepen, both participants must be willing to discover the values of the other person. As we learn these values, we will discover how much we are alike or unlike the other. Where we differ, we must at least attempt to understand the other person's values. This requires openness and honesty, and a willingness to accept what you learn about the other person even if you do not share her values.

If those values are non-moral, and thus not opposed to beneficial love, we should be careful not to respond in a negative way. It might take time for a person to feel the freedom to share who she truly is, but an atmosphere of acceptance prepares her for greater exposure. Without the freedom to open up and be discovered, we cannot please one another and our relationships will suffer from superficiality.

Communicate values

Until a relationship moves to conversation about values, you may find that you are not truly communicating. Even if you talk about your wants and desires, you still might not fully understand yourself or what you are wanting of the other person. And if you are speaking or acting from emotion then you might not be doing what is right for the relationship; you may only be seeking that which makes you feel good or happy. However, communicating your desires and emotions is still important because they give understanding into the values that you hold most deeply.

Truly knowing your values comes from comparing them to beneficial love so you can determine their effect on relationship. In non-moral areas of life, knowing your values according to the three areas of desire will help you communicate the deeper issues of your heart. Discussion using the framework of beneficial love and the three areas of desire will also make it easier for you to communicate in words that people can easily understand.

Especially in times of conflict, seek to list and communicate the values driving your desires, choices, and emotions. Although you still may not agree with each other (since everyone gives preference to different values), you will understand one another better, and you will more clearly communicate with one another.

In the workplace, conflict is more easily resolved when it becomes a discussion of values. The nature of the disagreement is better defined, and emotion can be kept in check. By communicating the foundational values of each side, resolution becomes an issue of changing the values that are conflicting.

If you have a child, attempt to understand the values behind his desires and actions. Talk to him about the values he holds, and discuss how they are similar or dissimilar to yours. Teaching your child that relationships are based on common value systems will help him understand the nature of his relationship with you, and it will also prepare him for having better relationships throughout life.

Help your child understand the three areas of desire so that he can make choices that will be best for his relationships with others, rather than only for himself. Children care deeply about what others think of them, even more than we who are older do. They need to know that good relationships are better than satisfying bodily appetites, having people like them, or being wealthy and powerful.

Guide your child to make relational decisions based on deeply shared values—both moral and non-moral. His long-term relational success requires a foundation deeper than emotion or an illusion of shared values. Once the reality of differing values becomes obvious, a strong foundation of beneficial love and shared interests will help sustain the relationship. Help him make wise relationship choices by discussing important life decisions prior to his engaging in life altering commitments.

Beneficial love can change you, it can change your

child, and it can change the world. As you and your child talk about values and how to sacrificially love those in your family, your family relationships will grow strong. Your family will share an identity of love that will be attractive to all those who live in conflict and heartbreak.

If you do not deliberately raise your child to share a common value system with you, he will likely choose one different than yours. That may lead to relational conflict—because all conflict in relationship is conflict over value system. Remember, you do not have to agree on everything. Rather, it is the foundation of beneficial love that is most important. If you seek to live sacrificially for one another, the other areas of interest that differ will not disturb the peace you share on the deepest level.

Recap:

- Truly knowing a person requires knowing her value system.
- Communication for resolving conflict should focus on values rather than desires and emotions.

Think:

- How will discussing my values make it easier to communicate my goals and desires?

8 Openness

The more time we spend with another person, the more opportunities we have for emotional experiences—both positive and negative. These experiences profoundly shape both the relationship and us. Therefore, we need to understand the long-term effect of emotions on relationship.

Over time, positive emotions bind us together and negative emotions drive us apart. Some relationships become entirely overwhelmed by negative emotions resulting in a complete breakdown of the relationship. Even in relatively good relationships that are free of constant conflict, closeness can diminish over time. This occurs because of times of negative emotion. All long-term relationships, such as those between a husband and wife, a parent and child, or among long-time friends, are subject to this effect.

Negative emotional reactions in relationships are a cue that something very important is occurring. They notify us about a choice we must make to prevent destroying the relationship slowly over time or immediately in a great explosion. To build a strong and deep relationship we must understand and manage these emotions through knowing our desires and the values that drive them.

The negative emotions that people experience in relationship are the result of their different value systems, even in small degrees. For example, a husband and wife might be talking together and the husband expresses an idea, thought, or dream that he has. If his wife makes a comment that causes him pain, either deliberately or in ignorance, he experiences a negative emotional reaction. Depending on the sensitivity of the one who is hurt, and by the intensity of his emotion, a choice may be made in that moment: "I will not speak with her about this again because she causes me pain." We feel crushed when our desire to be open is not met with acceptance, and over the course of a long-term relationship many such circumstances may occur.

This results in more and more of the person's heart becoming shut away from the other. Although there are still many areas of positive emotion, these episodes of negative emotional reaction cause him to close off portions of what truly matters to him. In this case, the accumulation of negative experiences does not cause a total breakdown in the relationship, but it does hinder the closeness in relationship that both desire. Damage to relationship is always the result of a difference in value system, even if a person disallows the expression of it verbally.

When we put up walls between us to protect ourselves from another person, we both lose. One loses the joy that comes from being open and loved for who he is, and the other loses the joy that comes from knowing him deeply. We desire to speak openly about what is in our hearts while still being accepted and loved, but negative emotions teach us to avoid it. This causes an inner struggle, usually accompanied by grief. Over time, relationships become boring because we believe we must hide important aspects of ourselves from one another.

In the human body, arteries carry fresh blood to each organ and limb providing the nourishment they need for good health. If these arteries become clogged, a portion of the body will die. Similarly, open communication over values is crucial to a relationship. Any time I refuse to discuss something that is important to another person, or if I disregard what is valuable to him, I clog a relational artery. Although the rest of the relationship may remain intact, *that* part of the relationship is in danger of dying. If too many parts of the relationship become clogged, or if I clog one that is significantly important, the entire relationship dies.

What ought to happen over time is a greater discovery of the other person. Constant openness and revelation keep relationships alive. When we have new experiences and are free to share our thoughts and reactions to them, the relationship grows deeper and more necessary for us. Of course, this presupposes we are not merely seeking confirmation of our selfish values.

There are reasons we do not honestly discuss our values. It may be because we are embarrassed, or that we are afraid we will not be accepted should our values become known. The person who has been hurt, and is now afraid to be open, values self-protection over openness and relationship. He is unwilling to have trusting love and to risk being open because of some past experience. He chooses to close off sections of his heart and refuses to discuss how the reactions of others have hurt him.

Therefore, we need to be careful and gentle with someone who is revealing his value system to us. We must not have an attitude of superiority or speak rashly against what we have heard. If we have said or done something that has negatively affected another person, we need to let him know that we love him and do not reject him. To share my value system is to share the deep issues of my heart; consequently, *rejection of my values is always perceived as a rejection of me.*

If we want others to be open and grow in relationship with us, we must be receptive to all that they are. When I counsel, I accept a person with the values he currently holds, without condemning him. We both know that he has come to me because he wants change in his life. My job is to identify the values that are causing problems, and guide the person to values that produce the outcomes he desires in relationship.

When someone is unable or unwilling to speak openly in a relationship, it is likely because both people have done something wrong. One currently refuses to be open because the other was previously hasty or uncaring in his words. In a growing relationship, discussing a problem will cause short-term pain for both individuals; but pain is normal as two people adjust to sharing a common value system. In a case such as this, both people need to change their values. This is often a difficult process, for one must be sacrificial in being open and willing to risk pain in order to extend the relationship, and the other must be sacrificial and love the other person regardless of what is being expressed.

Insecurity and openness in relationship

Insecurity is the feeling that we are losing someone's love. When a person is not doing our value system to us, we question if we are truly loved. Openness is regulated by the feeling of security we have in another person's love. Therefore, when we are open and share the deep values and secrets of our hearts, we need to have the other person treat those as valuable, too. If I hold something to be very valuable and I take the risk of being open and sharing it, I need the other person to demonstrate by her words and actions that she takes very seriously the value I place on it. If she does not regard it with my degree of value, it makes me feel hurt and unloved, causing me to want to close off that area of my heart.

The importance of openness is not only for husband and wife, but is especially crucial between parent and child. The issues our children face vary with their age, so we must begin early with them in cultivating an environment in which they feel safe sharing what is valuable to them. When their values need changing, we need to gently guide them toward beneficial love—love that is considerate of others. If we are abrupt with them, they will treat us as an unsafe audience and will keep their values a secret from us. Our influence with our children will then diminish until we regain openness with them.

Beneficial love is always open to hearing another's value system. Love desires to know the true person and accept him without condemnation. Love also desires to be open and share the matters of the heart. This explains why both people in relationship must have "risk-taking love" in terms of communication.

We need to exercise wisdom in relationship. Wisdom is primarily relational, for it primarily addresses how to maintain good relationships with other people. A wise person understands what is happening in the emotions, desires, and values of another. She is willing to discover and understand the other person and grow in relationship. In close relationships we must always remember that the other person is not perfect, even as we are not perfect. When someone opens up and shares a part of himself that is not perfect, he knows it is not perfect. If he shares a desire or dream, he knows that it is a desire or dream. Be very gentle with that part of someone's value system, even as you want others to be gentle with what you value.

The values that produce good emotions and strong relationships are love and honor. Sacrificial love for one another is open and accepting, not condemning and rejecting. It continues to be open even when it experiences hurt, and it accepts criticism even when mistreated. Otherwise, over time, relationships break down, fall apart, or simply become boring. To have great relationships we must have a great value system, and there is no greater value system than love that consciously considers the needs of others.

Recap:

- Negative emotions reveal a perceived rejection of our values.
- Rejected values are taken as a rejection of the value holder.
- When discussing values, people must be open and receptive.

Think:

- Which of my values am I afraid to share? Why?
- Is sharing them worth the risk of rejection?
- What would be the outcome of sharing my values and having them be accepted?

9 Emotions and Memory

Emotions play a critical role in the production of memory. The more intense the emotion, the more memorable the experience will be. Remembering such an event can reproduce the emotion associated with it because it remains connected to a deeply held value. As such, it is beautiful to observe an entire family reminisce about the happy memories associated with a loved one during a memorial service. Everyone recalls certain occasions because we most clearly remember events that correspond to our deepest values, whether positive or negative.

Memories can also be recalled and passed from generation to generation. Repeated stories, both positive and negative, affect family identity or the legends and myths of a people. They shape cultural attitudes and reinforce a people's value system. Thus, painful memories occupy not only the minds of individuals but also of groups.

While remembering pain can serve to protect us and keep us safe, pain and self-protection wreak havoc in relationships because painful memories lead to avoidance of deep relationship. If painful relationships cause us to avoid new ones, it can lead to depression since we are evading our greatest source of happiness: relationship.

Negative emotions produce self-protective behaviors, inhibiting our ability to act to benefit others. Instead of avoiding relationship, we must repair problems and remove hurt. Forming new, healthy relationships unlike past painful ones permits us to become free from fears related to past injuries.

The relational shame, disgrace, and pain that we feel can be alleviated. Some hurts and shame require an experience of openness, love, and special counsel because an injury is so deep that one cannot carry the pain alone. There is a power that offenses, committed both *toward* others and *against* us, continue to have as long as they remain hidden or secret. Talking about the painful event with a wise, loving, and trustworthy person often breaks this power.

If we were the ones who harmed someone, and we are no longer able to seek his forgiveness, we may have to admit this act to someone else in order to be free of the burden we carry because of it. Sometimes our consciences cannot be free until we have humbled ourselves before a trustworthy person who can assure us of loving acceptance. That person functions as an emotional representative offering loving forgiveness.

The best method for resolving painful memories established by negative emotion is through the relational tools of admitting fault, replacing values, forgiving, and reconciling. Painful experiences can be settled once those involved realize the source of the problem was one (or both) of their value systems, and forgiveness is offered by the injured party.

However, sometimes it is not possible to bring both parties together to resolve the problem and pain, either because a person is no longer present or because he is unwilling to discuss the matter. Occasionally we must wait patiently for a relationship to be restored, especially when waiting for someone to realize his fault.

Often someone who damages his relationships has first suffered through his own painful experiences. Attempting to understand the process by which he may have been injured allows us to create feelings of mercy and grace rather than bitterness. This allows us to avoid being emotionally scarred by him even if he is unwilling or unable to respond to us.

Dealing with past emotional pain is important because we need to be free of its negative relational effects. We must also never allow negative experiences from one relationship to adversely affect our other relationships. We must become people who are not enslaved by past emotional pain but are set free by love.

Recap:

- The more impact an action has on our value system, the deeper the memory associated with that action will be.

Think:

- Do my current relationships suffer from the emotional damage of past relationships?
- What steps can I take to resolve that pain and gain freedom?

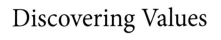

Discovering Values

10 Emotions Reveal Values

People attempt to change their negative emotions but are often unsuccessful because they do not understand what produces emotion. Because of this, their relationships often fail without their knowing why. In order to produce positive emotional change and repair relationships, we must first discover the values that dominate our lives. Then, as our values become more positive, we will experience greater joy in who we are, how we act, and how people react to us.

Emotions are like the tip of an iceberg, the visible portion of what lies hidden within the value system. Our emotional reactions are what we, and sometimes others, see. In order to change or understand our emotions, we need to go beneath the surface and address the values that motivate us. Emotions provide insights that allow us to understand all that we value and desire. They reveal what we believe is important even when we cannot consciously identify our true values.

What we value determines how we express our desires. When our desires are satisfied we have pleasant feelings and when our desires are frustrated we have unpleasant feelings. Thus, the fulfillment of our *values* determines our emotional responses to life and relationship. Remember, emotions do not reveal right and wrong; they only help us realize the intensity of our values and desires. Emotions do not reveal whether or not we *should* hold a value, only that we *do* hold it.

When our desires for happiness in relationship are thwarted or fulfilled, we experience emotion. Emotions that enhance relationship flow from living by the values of honor and love, whereas relationally destructive emotions result from selfish values. If we want good relationships that are emotionally fulfilling, we must embrace values that enhance relationship and relinquish damaging values.

We must have a goal and direction for what our values should become as we focus on changing them. If we do not, we will be dominated by our desires, driven on by our emotions, and make relationally destructive decisions. The conflicts we have in relationship are conflicts over values, and the negative emotions we experience in relationship are because of someone's selfish values. In order to resolve conflict, limit negative emotions, and control our desires, we must understand the selfish values that reside in our hearts so that we can change them. Without a change of value system, our lives and relationships will not improve.

Our emotions give us the ability to see within and discover the particular values that drive us. By understanding what is important to us, we can evaluate the positive and negative effects our values have on our relationships. Once we replace selfish values with ones that benefit others, our relationships will improve and produce more positive emotional feelings—both within ourselves and in the people we love.

11 Emotions and Our Bodies

We should not be surprised to learn that what happens to our physical bodies can have a significant impact on our emotions. Most parents quickly discover this about their children, and most husbands and wives can easily identify it in their spouses. There are many different physical factors that influence our emotions. Understanding this is important so that we do not become confused by physical causes of emotion while attempting to discover our values.

First, and perhaps the most significant, is our diet. Our emotions are affected not only by what we *do* eat but also by what we *do not* eat. Food and drink that may have a short-term positive effect on emotions, such as sugar or caffeine, often have a downside later. Conversely, the lack of certain nutrients in our diets can have a negative effect on us, as can dehydration from not drinking sufficient quantities of water.

The second physical factor affecting us is our need

for adequate rest and exercise. People react differently to lack of sleep, but constant weariness certainly degrades our moods. If we are not obtaining sufficient quality and quantity of sleep, it can have a dramatic effect on how we act toward one another. Short tempers often coincide with short nights.

A third negative cause is the amount of stress in our lives. Stress is not an emotion, but it can flow from several negative emotions. Physical stresses such as pain, lack of sunlight, and extreme temperatures should also be considered. Stress can also produce a circular cycle: negative emotions begin to have a negative effect on our physical bodies, which then leads to us having more negative emotions.

When trying to understand our emotions, we need to consider our physical environment. We must not blame our environment for our harmful responses to others, but we need to understand its effect on us. For example, when I become very tired late at night, I will occasionally become sad. However, being sleepy is not an excuse for being depressed; it is only a sign to me that I need to go to bed. In the morning I know I will feel fine again. Emotions of this type are cues for us to change our environments and to take care of our bodies.

There can also be physical problems where the biological systems of the body are over-producing or under-producing natural substances, and the body's systems are not functioning in proper balance. However, one must be wary of immediately turning to prescription drugs when the need for them is mere speculation rather than objective science. Otherwise, we might depend on drugs that allow us to continue living selfish values that damage our relationships without experiencing the negative emotions intended to drive us to change our values.

We must be careful to understand ourselves, and those around us, in terms of how we react to environmental stimuli. We must recognize our need to take care of ourselves through adequate sleep, nutrition, and exercise. We must also remember to be more gracious to others when their moods may be affected by physical causes, such as when they are tired or hungry.

Not only do our bodies affect our emotions, they also *react* to our emotions. When we are afraid or angry, our bodies prepare for fighting or fleeing. Our muscles tense and our heart rate is elevated as adrenaline enables us to respond to environmental stimuli, especially when we are in danger. We also know that happiness and laughter are physically good because positive emotions release natural chemicals that benefit us.

This positive physical reaction also occurs when we are around people who make us happy. The people we relate to really do produce physical reactions within us as they touch our value systems. This prompts us to gravitate toward people who produce positive emotions and to shy away from people who produce negative ones. However, we must never use this as an excuse for neglecting those we need to love.

A person's emotions, body, and mind are all interconnected. Therefore, we need to understand and regulate our emotions in order to avoid the physical toll caused by continuous exposure to negative ones. And, because addictions and damaging behaviors can be reinforced through positive feelings, the relational effects of our values must guide us, not the pleasures of a moment. Emotions cause us to pursue pleasure and to protect ourselves from danger and trouble. Since the outcomes of both can be either good or bad for us, we need to evaluate their long-term effects on our lives and relationships.

Recap:

- Our physical environment can impact our bodies and thus our emotions.

- We are drawn to people who produce positive emotions within us, and we avoid people who produce negative ones.

Think:

- Am I getting enough exercise and rest?

- Is my consumption of food, drink, and drugs negatively affecting my emotions?

- Does this affect my relationships?

12 Positive and Negative Reactions

Before we can fully understand our emotions, we must first understand the nature of emotional reaction. Usually, a single value within us drives at least two emotions. We feel a positive one when our value is achieved and we feel a negative one when it is thwarted. Therefore, in the following chapters, I have chosen to link emotions together by their natural connections to each another.

We label emotions as positive or negative depending on how they make us *feel*. Negative emotions are those generally associated with pain, frustration, or sadness, while positive emotions are usually associated with happiness or love. Regardless of whether you enjoy what you are feeling, any emotion—positive or negative—can have a good or bad result in your life.

We must be careful to understand that a right or good value system does not result only in positive emotion, and a relationally damaging one does not produce only negative emotion. Do not confuse the *outcome* of the emotion with whether or not the emotion is positive or negative. For example, anger can destroy a relationship, but it can also produce positive change in a relationship. Although both outcomes of anger share the exact same negative feeling, they have entirely different results.

We can also act in relationally destructive ways while having "positive" emotions. For example, an evil person can desire and take pleasure in that which is selfish or harmful to others. Furthermore, addictions can feel good while producing horrific personal and relational damage. Thus, values that are not good *can* produce short-term positive emotion. They are dangerous because the positive feelings reinforce negative behavior. Positive emotions result in healthy relational growth *only* if those emotions flow from good values.

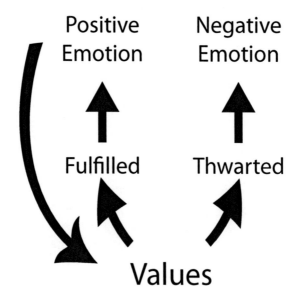

The end result of long-term negative emotion is depression. Depression is not an emotion; rather, it is the eventual outcome of several different emotions. It occurs when we feel overwhelmed by sustained negative feelings, especially when we also fail to find fulfillment in our relationships.

Since we find greatest happiness in life through relationship, loss of relationship produces our greatest sorrow. When relational failure produces more negative than positive emotion, we desperately seek substitutionary happiness through our appetites and personal domains.

My categorization of emotions and labeling them as negative or positive is certainly debatable. You may also disagree with my description or definition of each emotion. However, if you focus only on that aspect of my discussion, you will certainly miss my point. The idea I wish to convey is how you can use your emotional reactions as an indicator of your values.

As you consider each of the emotions discussed in the remainder of this book, attempt to understand the desires behind your emotions and the values that ultimately drive them. By constantly considering the issues of life according to the three areas of desire, you will gain insight into your value system and be able to change it to produce fulfilling relationships.

Simply put, we experience positive emotions when our value systems are fulfilled and negative emotions when they are not. Since, emotions are only a *response* to the underlying values and do not indicate whether the values are good or bad, we must never measure our values by how they make us feel. The only standard of measuring the goodness of an act for relationship is how it compares to beneficial love.

Recap:

- Positive emotions produce pleasurable feelings.
- Negative emotions result in avoidance behaviors.
- Emotions reveal values, not morality.
- Values, not emotion, produce relational stability.

Think:

- How have I pursued positive emotion that resulted in relational damage?

13 Boredom and Apathy

Although boredom and apathy are not emotions, they share a close connection to them. They are, in fact, the *opposite* of emotional experiences. But, since emotions serve a very important role in relationship, absence of emotion is a significant factor that must not be ignored. It is a sign that something is wrong.

Boredom

Boredom signifies a loss or absence of desire, and it should move us to pursue positive emotion. It is the abnormal condition of one who is not being driven by *positive* values. Boredom indicates absence of positive emotion flowing from the right value system. We may be bored because we are unable to seek the desires that we believe will bring us positive emotional pleasure, or because we are unwilling to pursue new and better values.

Lack of positive emotion stemming from good relational values can lead to seeking positive emotions through damaging values. Boredom without motion toward the pursuit of beneficial love opens one to seeking desires flowing from selfish values. If we are not pursuing positive emotions for doing what is good, we will eventually pursue positive emotions in doing what is wrong.

We can experience boredom in relationships, work, and leisure. The cure to boredom is to seek positive emotions resulting from beneficial love. Of course, this will fail if we are only attempting to *mimic* virtuous behavior without having first changed the values of our hearts. If we practice sacrificial love in relationship by serving others, we will be freed from both boredom and selfishness.

Apathy

I express apathy by saying, "I don't care." Sometimes when I say this, it is a conscious form of apathy: It is not that I *truly* do not care so much as I do not consider an issue worth investing in. Genuine apathy is different. Apathy is non-emotion. Apathy tells us that something means nothing to us. The absence of concern for what is happening reveals that we place *no value* on the outcome.

Genuine apathy for the welfare of others—being unmoved by human suffering—betrays a very selfish value system. Although we may feel powerless to act to meet the needs of others, our emotions should still reveal that we care. The cure for apathy is the same as the cure for boredom. Our values must change, and we must act according to beneficial love. We must believe people and relationships are valuable and act upon that belief.

Apathy and boredom both reveal that we are not pursuing positive emotions or living by values that produce healthy relationships. Their presence indicates selfish values that we need to address. We will experience positive emotions if we adopt and live values that produce good relationships. When we serve others in beneficial love, boredom and apathy retreat, our relationships improve, and we gain greater pleasure in relationship.

Recap:

- Boredom reveals lack of positive emotion.
- Apathy reveals diminished relational values.
- Pursuing relationships based on beneficial love cures both boredom and apathy.

Think:

- How would my helping someone cure a problem of boredom?
- How do I feel when others refuse to help me in my times of need?

14 Pride and Envy

You are familiar with the feelings of pride and envy and have already used them to evaluate your value system. Therefore, they serve as a good first example of how two emotions flow from the same underlying value. They are also two of the easiest emotions for understanding the connection between values, desires, and emotions.

Pride

Pride is not usually thought of as an emotion, and there are significant uses of the word "pride" that are clearly not emotion. However, there is an emotional aspect of pride, and I acknowledge this when I feel "proud of myself." I experience it when I think I have done something well because it is being happy with myself in connection to one of my values.

The source of this feeling can be either right or wrong: We can feel pride when we have done something good and have done it well, but we can also be proud of ourselves when we have done something selfish or evil. The emotion is the same either way, but the source of it is different. That is, the good *feeling* is present but the reason for it can be a good or evil value. Regardless, the emotion should make it easy for us to understand what is occurring within our hearts.

Consider what happens when we experience success: getting a great score on a test, winning a race or game, or being promoted at work. We are proud that we did well and we feel happy. There is nothing wrong with this feeling so long as the underlying activity is noble. Doing well at something that is good *should* make us feel good; it is our emotional reward for doing what is right.

However, being proud because we did something *better than others* is a different matter; we must not feel good or proud about that. When we do, we diminish others by taking pleasure in their subservience and internally gloat over our own superiority. It is not difficult to see why this attitude is relationally damaging: people do not like being regarded negatively.

Pride often reveals the desire to be served by others, to be greater than others, or to look good in the eyes of others. Although tied to the natural desire to be adored and have a good reputation, some underlying values of pride can destroy relationships. When we elevate ourselves over others without wanting to help them, we will not find happiness or admiration in relationship. However, if we excel *while serving others along the way*, people will recognize both our success and the honorable values that we possess.

Envy

We may not recognize the values behind pride because we are too preoccupied with feeling good to think about values. However, we are more attentive to envy since we are usually better aware of our negative feelings than our positive ones. Where pride is focused on self and blinds us to the true effect we have on others, envy screams at us making it difficult to ignore. We may be unaware of our pride, but envy does not go unnoticed.

Envy is the negative counterpart to the feeling of pride. It is the opposite of feeling good for a job well done. It is feeling bad or upset because someone else has done something better than we have. This emotion flows from the *exact same values* as the good feeling we get when we come out more favorably in our comparisons to others. When we "win" we feel good, but when we "lose" we feel terrible. If we have a problem with envy, we *also* have a problem with pride.

Envy is feeling bad when we finish in second place, or when someone "less" than us succeeds. Whether we measure others based on age, intelligence, gender, or some other factor, the real problem is that we value them less than ourselves and believe we should have life better than they do. The values producing envy must be determined in order to find the source of any ideas of entitlement.

These feelings flow from a wrong view of self. Finishing in second place still demonstrates that we have done well. But wrong values destroy moments of success. Instead of measuring what was actually achieved, there is a comparison of self to others. Envy at another's success causes us to make excuses about why we lost or why the other won. We complain, if only internally, and in that moment the value system we truly possess is revealed.

Pride and envy are felt according to the three areas of desire. We can envy the pleasures that others experience, how they look or succeed, or the amount of power and wealth they possess. Pride exalts self over others, flaunting its measure of success, while envy complains that life is not fair. We desire greatness, but requiring others to notice it destroys relationships. Pride and envy are both relational killers because they focus on self rather than on others.

The emotions pride and envy betray the love of pleasure, self-glory, and power. These reveal the values we consider more worthwhile than enjoyment of good relationship. Problems with pride and envy can be eliminated when we are motivated not solely for self, but also for serving others by helping *them* become successful.

Recap:

- Pride is relationally destructive when it flaunts victory over others.
- Envy cannot be pleased when others succeed.

Think:

- When has my desire for success damaged my relationships?
- When have I expressed envy when it was not truly warranted?
- What values does this expose?

15 Shame and Regret

Guilt is a legal term. It describes what we have or have not done. We are either guilty or not guilty. We either broke a law or we did not. Guilt is a legal status that has nothing to do with how we feel. We can be guilty, yet experience no feeling or emotion. This may occur through ignorance that an act was wrong, or through being taught something is permissible when, in fact, it is not. It can also happen if we do not believe that a decree is correct for determining right and wrong.

Shame, on the other hand, is the feeling associated with guilt. It occurs when we *believe* we have done something wrong, regardless of whether or not we have actually done so. This emotion is only a response to what I think is true; if I believe I have done something wrong, I will feel shame.

Shame provokes a range of emotional responses within us. Thus, we use a variety of words to describe the different aspects of shame. Although each one of them indicates the presence of different values, they all tightly revolve around issues of reputation and acceptance—the second area of desire.

The first form of shame concerns issues of modesty. Modesty is determined by culture and subculture; the people with whom we interact and where and when we live determine our ideas of what is appropriate. Every culture has rules of modesty, and we feel shame if we knowingly violate those rules. We may even feel shame merely by observing someone else violating our cultural standards.

Shyness is mild form of shame. It is discomfort with self in the present situation, being nervous because of what we imagine others think about us. This feeling arises from our desire to have people think positively about us. We experience shyness when we are unsure if others accept us since we are unaware of what they value. Shyness diminishes over time with people we know because we understand and grow comfortable within a circle of common values.

A third type of shame is the feeling of inadequacy. We experience this emotion when we believe we do not measure up to the value systems of others. In other words, we are measuring ourselves according to our understanding of another's value system. When we attempt to view ourselves as we think someone else sees us, and we feel that we do not measure up to that expectation, we feel inadequate. Where shyness was ignorant of the other person's value system, inadequacy knows what is valued and expects rejection.

Another kind of shame is embarrassment, and we usually mean this when we talk about shame. It occurs when we do not measure up to *our own* value systems. Our values dictate what we should be in action, word, or attitude; and embarrassment is our belief that we have failed to live up to that standard. We feel shame when we fail to achieve the ideals of our value systems in terms of body, relationship, and success. Shame proceeds from a contradiction between the values we profess and the values we actually possess.

We label others as having "no shame" if they live according to values permitting them much more freedom than our own. Someone may rarely experience shame because he has no difficulty measuring up to his value system: his personal standard is not very high. Conversely, those who are plagued with shame (feelings of guilt) do so because they have a great sense of difficulty in living up to their professed value systems. They have expectations of what they should do, be, or achieve, but they frequently find themselves unable to satisfy them.

Finally, there is self-pity. Self-pity is feeling shame while blaming others for it. That is, emotions relating to shame are felt and we consider it someone else's fault. Self-pity is inner conflict produced from holding values we do not wish to possess.

The solution to shame

Pursuing values that you believe are wrong results in shame, so you must either change the values generating shame or modify your beliefs about what is right and wrong. Not every value we possess is good for relationship, and not every moral guideline imparted to us is true. We must be careful to choose wisely whether we are acting against a relationally good value, or need reject a moral value taught to us.

Even as two people have conflict in relationship when they possess different value systems, inner conflict arises when we attempt to *change* our own value systems. Until we resolve the issue of which values we will adopt and follow, we will continue in a troubled state. We have difficulty "living with ourselves" when we are violating one or more of our own values; and without change we will continue to act on conflicting values that produce inner turmoil and, potentially, shame.

In order to remove feelings of shame resulting from wrong actions toward others, there are two steps that must be taken. First, we must admit our fault and replace the values producing the shame. Of course, movement toward beneficial love is important: values supporting and proceeding from beneficial love will not produce shame. You will never feel bad about helping another person, so long as you are not being exploited in the process.

Second, we must accept forgiveness offered to us. Once the relationship is restored to a healthy state based on right values, feelings of shame begin to diminish. When we forgive someone, we extend to them grace and mercy; we need to extend that same grace and mercy to ourselves when others forgive us. If someone has forgiven you, it means they have judged you and *still* loved you enough to release you from the relational debt you owe.

There is a danger in punishing yourself for an act done to another, and for which you have been forgiven. Although you feel bad for what you have done, it was not done *to* you. You cannot "forgive" yourself because the offence was not committed against you. Your only remedy is receiving forgiveness from outside of yourself, and once you receive that forgiveness you must not keep punishing yourself. Do not judge yourself more harshly than the one who has forgiven you.

Regret and remorse

Although many consider feelings of regret or remorse as negative, they can actually be very constructive experiences because of their effects. The feelings are definitely not pleasant, but the nature of regret is positive. Regret and remorse are nearly synonymous, although remorse is stronger and is usually accompanied by a sense of guilt.

Regret is a feeling directly related to shame. Shame is the embarrassment of a moment; although it might linger or be felt again each time we remember an uncomfortable situation. However, regret can subsequently provoke shame for an act that initially produced no shame or embarrassment.

We can regret feeling ashamed or we can regret the action for which we feel shame. This explains why someone can be sorry about being caught while not being sorry for what he has done. He regrets being caught but does not regret what he was caught doing.

Remorse differs from shame in that it feels sorry for the *consequences* of an action: It is a desire for another outcome. Whenever we wish we had acted differently—*by different values*—we are being moved by remorse. Remorse often considers how personal actions affected other people, and wants to take them back.

Regret is evaluative. It seeks to measure the outcome of a value system. It looks at life and considers what happened to me, to my status, or to my possessions. It asks *why* something happened: "Why am I like this? Why do people treat me as they do? Why is my domain such as it is?" Regret looks at the answers to those questions and does not like what it sees. Regret wants different outcomes.

Therefore, regret precipitates value change. At least, that is what it should accomplish. Otherwise, we are doomed to repeat our mistakes or turn to self-pity and blame others for our problems in life. Sometimes we later regret previous decisions that seemed right at the time. This redefining of "right" reveals the shifting nature of our values.

We regret that which harms our body, our reputation, and our domain. We regret the outcome of over-eating but not the pleasure during indulgence. We want people to like us and cheer for us even if our actions do not deserve it. We fight with our spouse or parents in order to have our own way at home, but regret the damage caused to our relationships. *We want to fulfill our value systems without suffering the negative consequences of them.*

Regret and remorse are powerful emotions intended to help us change our values, but they only produce better relationships once coupled with the right value system. Although the results of our actions cannot be separated from the values producing them, we often prefer to fulfill our own desires rather than say "no" to them for the sake of others. All regret in relationships can be mitigated by seeking to benefit others rather than seeking to please only self.

Regret produces value change, but the direction it takes us depends on the new values we adopt to replace the old ones. Do we regret that we did not satisfy ourselves, receive recognition and attention, and self-gain? Do we only regret the outcomes of what we do, or do we also regret the selfish values behind our actions? Desires fulfilled in the context of beneficial love result in good relationships without the sourness of shame and regret.

Recap:

- Shame is the result of not measuring up to your own value system.

- Regret evaluates life and helps us change our values to produce better outcomes in future circumstances

Think:

- How will my feelings of shame diminish if I seek beneficial love as my dominant guiding value?

- Would shame in my relationships be resolved if I was loved beneficially?

- Have I changed the underlying values that have caused me regret?

- Have I sought to restore relationships that I regret damaging?

16 Sadness and Happiness

Two of the simplest and strongest indicators of whether or not we are achieving our values are sadness and happiness. Our responses can be subtle or sublime, but we would be foolish to ignore how much these emotions can teach us about ourselves. Whether we are amused or disappointed, our values are speaking to us.

Sadness

We experience a range of emotion related to sadness, including disappointment, grief, and despair. Some of these are genuine feelings of sadness from legitimate sources, but at other times we punish ourselves by deliberately remaining sad and refusing comfort because we believe we deserve to feel bad. Occasionally we may feel sad but be unsure why. Of course, there is always a reason even if we are not aware of it at a conscious level. It may be a need for rest or something in our diet, but more than likely it springs from one or more of our values.

Disappointment is a mild sadness derived from unmet expectations of self, others, or situations. It is the first indicator that valued outcomes in life have failed to materialize. Disappointment often precedes anger, and an angry person usually began as a disappointed person.

Grief is a form of sadness that occurs when we experience loss. It is associated with the belief that something precious can never be recovered. Of course, this expresses the loss of something we valued deeply. When it is a loss of a person or relationship, special occasions and anniversaries become enduring reminders of that value.

Despair is feeling that life will never be good again. When deep sadness overwhelms us over a period of time, we can forget how life was without it. Despair is the loss of hope, and people who have lost hope often believe they will never be happy again. When people lose hope they become very susceptible to destructive behaviors because they believe nothing matters anymore. Unresolved despair leads to depression or suicide.

Sadness can also be felt *for* others: empathy is feeling emotions based on the circumstances of others. However, we need to be aware that the emotion we feel is based on *our own* values and not the other person's. Although we *assume* others react as we would, given their difficulty, someone may not experience the same degree of sadness as us since she possesses a different value system, whether formed previous to her hardship or because of it.

The source of sadness

Experiencing sadness should cause us to consider dissatisfaction with regard to the three areas of desire and the values driving them. Disappointment is not merely a result of unsatisfied appetites; it is a result of thwarted values. The degree of sadness indicates how important the underlying issues are to us.

If our desire to be admired, adored, or loved goes unfulfilled, or if people do not treat us as we want to be treated, we might become sad. Similarly, if our status is not at the desired level, or if we have been mistreated, snubbed or hurt by others, we might become sad or depressed. The desire to have people like us, and *value us as much as we value ourselves*, often leads to disappointment in our relationships.

We become sad and disappointed when our desires to have power, control, and wealth are not met. It may be as simple as not reaching the goals we have set for ourselves, regardless of whether or not they were realistic. Worse, we can experience despair when we feel powerless in a relationship or at work, or when we believe we have failed at something important.

The cure for sadness requires tracing the sadness to the source value. Be aware that possessing the right value system does not guarantee that we will be happy all the time. If we love people, we cannot avoid sadness during some of life's circumstances. We all experience sadness, loss, and suffering regardless of our value systems.

Sometimes we feel sad because of other people's problems; we are sad because we want a better life for them. This may even be an issue of control if we erroneously believe that we could fix the problems in their lives if only we were more powerful. Yet, sadness over the circumstances of others can have a positive outcome if we work to make the lives of others better. It can motivate us to stop living only for self and seek to meet the needs of others less fortunate than ourselves.

Sadness is not necessarily a sign that a value needs to change, since loving others sometimes naturally results in sadness. However, an unhealthy avoidance of sadness often leads people to shun relationship or choose only shallow, temporary ones. This fear of sadness causes many to miss both the goodness and happiness of relationship.

Happiness

Happiness is one of the prime motivators of all people. We desire to be happy and we do that which we believe, at least in the moment, will make us happy. We also want those we love to be happy. Feelings of happiness are usually described with words such as amusement, contentment, satisfaction, peace, and elation. Happiness is the direct result of having your desires and values fulfilled.

A person can be happy if his appetites are satisfied. This is the initial source of addictions. Basically, addictions are a way of seeking happiness in a bodily appetite. For example, eating food makes us feel happy so we often eat more food, and more frequently, than our bodies require. As with any bodily appetite, the positive feelings associated with its fulfillment are only temporary. If we cloak negative feelings caused by our selfish values with pleasures obtained from bodily appetites, it is only a matter of time before we are slaves to those appetites. Instead of fixing problems, addictions add a new layer of relational difficulty.

Being "in love" also produces chemicals within us that make us feel good and happy. Unfortunately, many people chase after this feeling even if it requires abandoning a current relationship. They are addicted to a chemically induced feeling of excitement when they should be seeking happiness in stable relationships. They exchange long-term happiness and peace for temporary highs.

Others become discouraged once the "in love" feeling diminishes and their happiness with a relationship begins to fade. If one's relationships are measured by this feeling instead of common values, a person is doomed to cycle through many heartbreaks. There is a depth of relationship that comes only from sharing life experiences and expressing the deep values of the heart with someone who has proven trustworthy and faithful long term.

We are happy when we believe people like us, and we feel good when we are admired and adored. We crave attention, and often act primarily to cause others to approve of us. To achieve that, we give others what we think they want from us, from a friendly look to a generous gift. The "class clown" acts to receive attention while hoping to be liked for his antics, athletes can be motivated by prestige, and academicians like to be known for how intelligent they are.

Much of what we do is governed by what other people—even strangers—think of us. Many of our behaviors show we are deeply motivated by the desire to be part of a group. Sometimes we are tempted to participate in an activity for the sake of approval rather than do what we know is right. Awareness of this weakness allows us to live by values that are good for relationship, rather than reacting to how others respond to us or treat us.

Happiness can also be felt by accumulating possessions and wealth, and by having people serve us according to how we feel we deserve to be treated. Shopping makes us happy because it satisfies our current desires for new clothes or toys. However, happiness in domain is transient, which explains how some people never seem to have enough money, possessions, or power.

Ultimately, we are happy because we are achieving our values. Our value systems are most often revealed by happiness. But, as with pride, we are often too preoccupied with happiness to think about our values, especially when our current enjoyment is in something we know is wrong. Contrary to popular thought, it is better to be good than to feel happy.

Much of the time, given the choice between being happy and being good, we choose to be happy. But happiness found in values that exploit others will never bring permanent happiness, and it is also relationally destructive. Happiness shared with another is dependent on our having and living a mutually beneficial value system. If we are motivated by the right values, the experiences of bodily appetites, human relationship, and personal possessions will bring deep satisfaction and contentment.

Do not confuse feeling good with being good

We need to pause for a word of caution. *Emotions do not teach us anything about whether our values are right or wrong.* We can be happy about what is wrong and sad about what is truly good. The emotions we experience only reveal whether or not something is *important* to us. They only reveal whether or not we are receiving or achieving the desires that flow from our value systems.

Do not use a feeling to determine what is right or wrong. Feeling good about something does not make it right, and feeling bad about something does not make it wrong. The emotions are positive and negative, but that does not determine whether the underlying value is positive or negative for relationship.

Furthermore, our value systems are composed of what we *think* is right or wrong. The beliefs behind our values are formed through what we have been taught about good and evil or about what others want us to do. But what we believe or have been taught may not be good for relationship. In order to evaluate values, we need to analyze their effect on relationship and not merely how they make us feel.

The primacy of relationship

People experience happiness according to the three areas of desire: appetites, reputation, and domain. But, because the second one is predominantly relational, it has the greatest potential to affect happiness and sadness. Once our damaged relationships produce more sadness than happiness, we seek satisfaction in bodily appetites and possessions, generating a cycle away from healthy relationships.

Fulfillment of all three areas of desire can be found in a healthy relationship and can bring us the greatest happiness. But, in order to have relationships that produce more happiness than sadness, we must practice values that enhance relationship. When we live by beneficial love, which is primarily relational, our relationships will bring us more happiness than if we practice selfish values.

Of course, the fullest extent of this happiness can only be experienced when those we live with are *also* attempting to love us beneficially. When two people both seek sacrificial love for the other they will be happy together, but when one or both individuals begin seeking happiness in what is selfish and destructive the relationship suffers and begins to die.

People need to be fully aware of their own expectations of what will produce happiness for them. Lives dominated by the pursuit of happiness in appetites and domain, rather than good relationships, reveal that there are areas of relationship in need of restoration. If our lives are characterized by sadness, our relational values need to be evaluated and replaced.

Most often, sadness enters our lives because we seek happiness in what ultimately damages our relationships. Pursuing happiness, we frequently seek immediate gratification of our desires in appetites, admiration, and personal domain *even when they harm relationship.* Although the desires are not wrong, happiness is transient when driven by relationally destructive values.

Happiness and sadness are powerful indicators revealing how we feel about the relationships we are in, and they can be used for discovering the parts of our hearts that need to be transformed. Of all the emotions, happiness and sadness most clearly express how we feel about the quality of our relationships—a quality that depends on how well we are practicing beneficial love.

Recap:

- Sadness is not necessarily a sign that a value needs to change, but it does express our disappointment that a value has not been met.

- Happiness is not a measure of virtue, it simply reveals if we are achieving our values.

Think:

- When was I happy about something that was not good?

- Do my relationships produce more happiness or sadness for me?

- Which of my values are exposed by my feelings of happiness?

17 Love, Loneliness, and Jealousy

Many of us are strangers to the emotion we call love. We have experienced it, but we usually do not experience it often or continuously. This feeling of love may also be described as romance: It is how we feel when we are "in love" with someone.

Our culture makes much of love as a feeling, but love is not merely a feeling. Part of our confusion arises from having so many different uses for the word love. The truest form of love is sacrificial *action* for the benefit of others. Although that action can produce the feeling we call love, we can also muster the love emotion in the absence of other people.

The emotion of love has two aspects to it. First, there is the emotion of being loved; that is, how we feel when someone loves us. I call that "incoming love." Second, there is the emotion of loving someone; that is, how we feel when we believe we love someone. I call that "outflowing love." They are related but different.

Incoming love

There are different *levels* of the emotions we experience when we feel love. At the most intense level, we can have a "madly in love" feeling; and, at the lowest level, we might simply be pleased that someone, even a stranger, let us ahead of them in the grocery line. These emotions function as two extremes with the same source.

There are also many *aspects* to this feeling of being loved. Feeling loved can relate to our safety and security, and it can be having our physical appetites and our emotional needs met. With love, numerous parts of us are touched, both internally and externally.

We experience the feeling of being loved when someone does something to us, or for us, that pleases us. Words without action do not convince us that we are loved; and, since we must believe we are loved for us to experience emotion, we must trust the other person is acting with honest and good intentions toward us.

Outflowing love

The second emotional part of love is the emotion we feel when we love someone else. This can be an extreme feeling of love for another person, or simply self-satisfaction that we acted kindly toward someone in need. The kinds of emotions and the extent to which we feel them depend on the nature of the relationship. We have one type of emotion toward a spouse, another regarding our parents and children, another for friends, and still another kind toward strangers for whom we have empathy or pity. It can be a subtle feeling of affection toward a child, or simply goodwill to a neighbor. At it's most extreme, love for someone can result in being flustered and overwhelmed by emotion when in the presence of the object of affection.

Strong feelings of love toward someone we barely know can often be confusing. This sensation of "being in love" is a pleasurable combination of happiness and hormones that we can feel even if the other person does not know we exist. Thus, outflowing love can occur solely *in the mind* regardless of any action, reality, or reciprocation. Knowing this will help us understand the true nature of this emotion.

Because many people equate love with the emotion we call love, they also speak of losing "that loving feeling." They may say that they have "fallen out of love" or "I don't love him anymore." Of course, what they often really mean is that the strong emotion is no longer present. This explains why it is important to continuously stress the idea that love is not only a feeling but also an act of the will.

However, if emotions reveal what is important to us, we must understand this emotion that plays such a large role in our relationships. We must understand why we have these emotions of loving and being loved. Gaining understanding of them gives us insight and clarity into why we feel "in love" or why we no longer feel our relationship is as romantic as it once was.

Love and value systems

Unsurprisingly, our emotions regarding love have everything to do with our value systems. We desire to have our values fulfilled for our benefit, and we want people to do what we value. Therefore, we feel loved when others do what *we* desire. When we feel incoming love, it is because another person is doing *our* value system *to us*.

The more important a fulfilled value is to us, the stronger our emotional feeling of being loved. The emotions of love require incoming actions that substantiate words because we do not truly feel loved unless someone other than self fulfills our values and makes us *believe* we are loved. Conversely, when the opposite of what we value is done, we feel unloved. When someone acts against our value systems, it hurts us; and the depth of that injury is directly related to the importance we place on the value connected to it.

Any feeling of love, whether major or minor, is also connected to the fulfillment of our bodily appetites, our desire to be adored, or our desire to be in control. Since every value is expressed or touched by those three areas, it explains the commonality that exists in what it means to feel loved. Yet there are also differences unique to each one of us since no one perfectly shares the same value system.

We feel loved when someone meets our values in the three areas of desire, but of the three areas, our need for recognition and adoration has the most bearing on relationship. Although the other two areas are significant, knowing that we are loved and adored for *who we are* counters feelings of rejection produced by differences in other parts of our value system.

The desire for recognition is a huge part of the human condition, resulting in the need to often hear that we are loved, adored, and special to others. It is why we typically do not believe others admire us unless if we can confirm it in ourselves. And, it is also why we must first *believe* someone loves us before we can gain the emotional benefit of feeling loved by him or her. In other words, *it is much easier to feel that you love someone than for you to feel that they love you.*

Our emotion of being loved is dependent on incoming love—someone doing our value systems to us. I feel loved when someone fulfills my bodily appetites in the way I desire. I feel loved when someone adores me and likes me. I feel loved when someone meets my desires for power, control, and possessions. When others accomplish my value system for me, I feel happy; and being happy in relationship is the emotion we call love.

When we practice outflowing love—doing others' value systems to them—they feel loved. However, doing *your own* value system to others may not result in their feeling loved. It all depends on whether or not you share the same values. The closer two people are in value system, the easier it is for them to love each other and the more consistent their feelings of loving and being loved. Romance is all about shared value system in relationship.

Let us examine a typical person's value system regarding the emotion of "being in love" and consider what happens when a person begins to have that "loving feeling." To make it more interesting, we will use an imaginary couple, Tim and Karen. When they first meet, they will have little understanding of each other's value system.

Initially, Tim imagines that Karen meets the desires of his value system. He also imagines that she believes that he can meet her desires. Finally, and most importantly, Tim believes that he and Karen share many of the same values. Without knowing much about Karen, except perhaps her physical appearance, Tim already sees the two of them as a match *in value system*. Tim's feelings of being "in love" are pure imagination at this point, but time will dissipate his delusion.

The biggest part of Tim's value system that he desires to share is Tim himself. He wants life to revolve around him. He wants his needs met. And he wants to be happy. Unsurprisingly, Karen has those same values, but centered on Karen rather than Tim. Initially, it is easy to focus all your attention on another person, making him or her feel loved. But as each one discovers that the other person's value system has a lot more to do with self rather than the other, they begin to lose some of that loving feeling.

Over time, it becomes apparent that they had *projected* their own value systems on to the other. That is, they assumed that their values were alike but became disappointed with the other person as they discovered the differences. Since relationship is built on a common value system, it was easy for Tim to enter that relationship when he presumed Karen's value system was like his. However, when he discovered the reality of her different values, the relationship began to break down, and the emotional feelings shifted from positive to negative.

When I feel that I love someone, I will do *my own* value system to her more naturally than I do *her* value system to her. Thus, I can *feel* that I love her and I may even be doing loving actions toward her (according to my definitions), but she still may not feel loved by me. This is because my actions are based on what makes *me* feel loved according to my values rather than by her values.

In order for two people to connect and both feel the emotion of love, they must have a clear understanding of *both* of their value systems. You must not only know your own value system, but also the value system of the other person. As you grow together in relationship by converging in value system, your ability to understand and practice the other person's value system—and thus love them—also grows.

However, two people may share many of the same values but still not have the emotion of love. This can occur either because they do not share their most important values, or because of conflicts that arise in other areas of their value systems. Although we might share many values, I need my most important ones met. When I feel unloved it is because I believe that others are not meeting my value system. I am measuring how they care for my physical needs, how they demonstrate their adoration of me, or whether they are giving me my own way and that which I desire. If the most important values underlying these three areas are not addressed, I will lose the emotion of love.

Even though we may share many common values, feelings of love are diminished because of conflicts that arise in other areas. Relationship and emotions are all about value systems, so even little issues of value system can destroy loving feelings. The loss of emotion stems from a growing knowledge of the *differences* in value system. When we hurt one another because of conflict in our values, it produces pain and sadness. If we feel misunderstood or rejected, we learn to hide our true values which denies us the possibility of having those values met by the other person.

Any difference in value system creates some degree of tension or conflict. When life is not as we prefer, we feel that we are not loved. Instead, we begin to think that others are more concerned with themselves than with doing this "one small thing" for us. For example, a husband and wife may share many common values regarding life goals and morality. However, other unshared values can destroy loving feelings, especially when actions repeatedly bring these differences to mind. Even relatively unimportant acts (such as dirty laundry on the floor, toothpaste "incorrectly" squeezed, cupboard doors left open, or lights left on) produce agitation that over years can diminish positive emotions and adversely affect the relationship.

Unless there is greater happiness from other positive experiences in the relationship, one or both people will begin to lose their loving feelings. If this can occur over minor issues, even more permanent damage is caused by fighting, arguing, and extreme conflict. The issues that cause the anger and frustration must be dealt with through admitting fault, replacing values, forgiving, and reconciling. Most importantly, selfish behavior must be replaced with consistent loving action or the relationship will slowly die.

We become more disappointed with another person as we discover how dissimilar we truly are and how we really do not share all the same values. Over time, all relationships experience these disappointments. That is why it is easier to *feel* more in love with those whom we have newly met. We are still unaware of how different they are from us; and we have not yet experienced much, if any, disappointment with them.

Some of what we desire is neither right nor wrong. There is no right or wrong way to squeeze the toothpaste tube, yet our belief about it is a part of who we are. However, the real issue is how we act toward others. What is right or wrong is how willing we are to serve another person in love. What is right or wrong is how much we seek to maintain a loving relationship even when we have conflict over non-moral values.

Restoring loving feelings

In order to repair the damage done to relationship, both participants must adopt the common value system of beneficial love. Each must also develop a clear understanding of what the other believes is important. This requires open communication of one's own desires and values, and being receptive to what the other believes is valuable. From that understanding, they can begin to love each other sacrificially.

Sacrificial love means seeking to do what I know makes another person feel happy and loved. I must change my selfish values that damage relationship and modify my behavior if I know I regularly do something that annoys my loved one. I also need to focus on how the other person fulfills my most significant values, rather than focus on the trivial items that bother me or are left undone.

If a husband and wife want to restore romance to their relationship they must both seek to have sacrificial love for each other. If only one pursues sacrificial love while the other remains selfish, relationship problems will not be resolved. Where significant damage has been done to the relationship, fault must be confessed so that emotional healing can begin. A couple will never solve issues of annoyance and restore romance if one or both partners refuse to seek the good of the other and continue to bring conflict to the relationship.

As both begin to live in beneficial, outflowing love, it will become natural for them to do to the other person what they want done in return. Since they share the same core value, outflowing love and incoming love coincide. This will not encompass every desire and interest in life, but it will resolve most relationship conflict. Thus, two people seeking to sacrifice for each other form a beautiful and strong relationship.

Without honest and open discussion of the values driving bodily appetites, adoration, and domain, a person may not learn which of his desires is reasonable and which is selfish. One cannot be blamed for being unloving when the values and desires of the other person remain hidden. If something is important to you, you must risk exposing that value or it will forever remain unfulfilled.

If something can be done to serve another according to what she deems important, you must be willing to do what makes her happy in the relationship. However, as you do her value system to her, you must also seek to have her become a sacrificial lover. You must not allow her to become a selfish monster by allowing yourself to be exploited.

When the little aspects of life begin to bother us, we have a few options. We can choose to experience negative emotions, such as anger or sadness, relating to unfulfilled values and desires, or we can overrule our value systems with more powerful values or desires. Instead of focusing on a minor area of frustration, we must set our minds on that which is more important to us: the relationship we desire to achieve with the other person and our desire to have sacrificial love for them.

The feeling of love is dependent on the act of beneficial love. Incoming love requires a belief in the mind that another person is acting for our good, and it looks for the ways that belief is proven to be true. Outgoing love is demonstrated by acting for the benefit of the one we love. It results in positive emotion when it is met with a thankful response (verbal or non-verbal) to the sacrifice given for the other person's benefit.

Loving our children

Most of my previous illustrations relate to husband and wife relationships, but these ideas of love apply similarly to all other relationships. If we want to make a child (or anyone else) feel loved, we need to follow the same steps. We need to demonstrate love to the child according to the same three areas that are important to us: appetites, reputation, and domain.

Parents must meet the physical needs of their child. This goes beyond food and clothes and includes touching, hugging and holding them. Parents must let their children know that they are proud of them, pleased with them, and that they enjoy them. Children feel our love when our words encourage them and we applaud their successes. Parents must create strong family bonds by giving each child a role in the family's "kingdom." They love it when we listen to their dreams and share the excitement they have for their activities and future. We must demonstrate how much we value what they value and encourage them to speak freely about what is in their hearts.

If you fail to meet the legitimate values of your child, she will seek to have her values fulfilled by those outside your family. She will be susceptible to exploitation, mistaking true love with an inadequate substitute. If you do not take your child's dreams seriously, someone else will. He will have more influence in your child's life than you do because he is forming a relationship with her over values that you have rejected. This is most serious when non-moral values become a bridge to her adopting moral values you reject.

The value systems of children are as complex as those of adults. There are aspects that are both good and selfish, and it is not always easy for us to understand all that transpires within them. Therefore, as you meet your child's needs, take care to also train him to love beneficially so that she learns how to cultivate strong relationships and develop a desire to meet the needs of others.

Loneliness

With a clear understanding of love, loneliness becomes very easy to understand. Loneliness develops from a sense of loss. The loss may be imagined, or there might be something truly missing. Nostalgia is a mild form of this, but it is usually broader in scope than loneliness, which has to do with relationship. Personal loneliness springs from feeling unloved or from the loss of loving emotions.

Loneliness occurs when we feel that those closest to us do not truly love us according to our own value systems. Even within a relationship we may feel alone in what we value, forcing us to hide the deepest parts of who we are. Loneliness is the belief that we have no one in our lives to love us and meet our deepest values. If being loved is having someone know, accept, and fulfill our values, loneliness comes from a real or imagined rejection of our values and, therefore, us.

Practicing beneficial love can often resolve loneliness. Values that produce loneliness are often selfish or at least *focused* on self; but once we change them and begin looking for opportunities to help in the lives of others, we find happiness and freedom in healthy relationships. The natural outcome of loving others sacrificially is involvement in the lives of others, which produces new relationships and brings fulfillment of positive values.

Jealousy

Jealousy is not purely negative; however, the experience of it is negative. That is, there can be good reasons for being jealous, and positive outcomes from it, but the feeling of jealousy is always unpleasant. Jealousy is the fear of losing one's place in another's life. This fear of being replaced has two aspects to it, relating to both outflowing and incoming love.

First, jealousy fears that someone else will take our place in fulfilling the values and desires of the one we love. The strongest feelings of jealousy arise when we fear that our replacement will fulfill our loved one's needs better than we do. Jealousy derives from the belief that we are unacceptable at fulfilling our loved one's value system.

Second, jealousy fears that incoming love will diminish or cease with the loss of our role in our loved one's life, resulting in loneliness. With jealousy, we can fear losing both the object of our love *and* fear the loss of receiving love. Jealousy makes us feel unlovable and unworthy, and it screams that our values will not be fulfilled. We feel jealous because we fear that we can be replaced and that our replacement will receive the love we currently enjoy. Thus, jealousy is an emotion resulting from our desire to be loved.

Jealousy does not want to share the object of love with another. One of the core values in an exclusive relationship (e.g. a marriage) is a desire to be the only one who meets certain needs for the other. Each one enjoys, desires, and needs to be the one who makes the other person feel happy and loved. Jealousy is about exclusiveness, and it does not want someone else to fulfill the incoming love needs of our beloved. Jealousy expresses our values relating to insecurity, inadequacy, and fear.

How does a lover prevent jealousy in the one he loves? He must cultivate within her the belief that she is loved and will never be replaced. Even though aspects of others may be lovely, the loved one will never be replaced or experience diminished love. He needs to let her know that she alone meets his needs in ways that no one else can or ever will. She needs to know that she makes him feel loved by fulfilling his values and desires.

Increasing relational depth can prevent jealousy. If my loved one meets all of my most important values, there will be no longing to have them met by anyone else. However, without honest and open communication and the desire to fulfill one another's needs, we cannot be sure that we are moving toward, rather than away from, each other.

We feel *loved* when someone fulfills our values, and we feel *loving* when we do our value systems to others. The concept is simple but understanding the depths of our hearts is not. The emotions of love, loneliness, and jealousy help us understand our desires, which in turn help us understand our true values. Understanding and openly sharing our desires and values allows us to become better lovers who are able to successfully cultivate the emotion of love in others.

We must be careful to evaluate whether what we desire and value produces good relationships. Although it is better to love beneficially than to have the emotion of being "in love," many people would rather experience this temporary feeling than a fulfilling long-term relationship. However, if our relationships are established on right values, we can have good relationships as well as good feelings.

Recap:

- Emotions of love are produced when we believe we love or are loved by someone.
- Sacrificial action allows our words of love to have real meaning to the one we love.
- Loneliness arises from the belief that we have no one to fulfill our values and needs in a loving relationship.
- Jealousy arises from the fear that a loving relationship is in danger.

Think:

- How to I measure my love for those closest to me?
- Is this the same measure they use to evaluate my love?
- Do I back up my words of love with sacrificial action?
- Do I thank those who love me for their specific acts of love?

18 Anger and Disgust

Anger and disgust are negative emotions. They do not feel good to us, but they can be very powerful motivators for good in our lives. However, if we do not understand them, or if they flow from selfish values, they can quickly destroy our relationships.

There are many different degrees of anger, most of which are related to an offense against ourselves or someone else. However, anger can also be a reaction to disappointment at not getting our own way. It can be as mild as frustration or as dramatic as rage, at which point the emotional state is so extreme that words and actions may occur without thought.

Resentment is anger that resides in the mind, characterized by reoccurring thoughts of an offense that may be accompanied by ideas of revenge. Unchecked, it leads to bitterness, which is a feeling of being angry "all the time." Although it may be a low level anger, it is a bitter person's constant companion. When a person is bitter, his anger often overflows to other people and situations, and he has difficulty acknowledging the connection to the original issue. Almost everything in a bitter person's life becomes bothersome.

Hatred is a strong form of anger directed specifically against another person. When a man's heart is full of hate, he desires or seeks to harm the object of his anger. Hatred yearns for the suffering and misery of another person. Enmity is mutual hatred between two people or groups; it is the most difficult kind of anger to resolve.

Why do we become angry?

Anger arises from a strong belief that something is not as it should be: an aspect of life is not the way it *ought* to be, or another person is not acting in the way he ought to act toward us or someone else. The crucial element to remember is that the feeling of anger flows from our value systems. It flows directly from our belief about what life should be like regarding rightness or justice, especially when we perceive a wrong has been done.

Fortunately, anger usually contains hope that the problem can be fixed. Whereas despair causes us to believe that the problem will not change, anger seeks to work toward a solution. Therefore, in order to understand our anger, we need to look for the *difference* between what is happening and the values we hold. Anger reveals what we believe is wrong and what we think needs to be changed, and should direct us toward the problem we want to correct.

Unfortunately, although seeking good outcomes, angry people do not always use methods that preserve relationship. Instead of seeking to change values, they sometimes focus their anger against other people. We must not direct our anger toward people as though they are simply a problem to be fixed or removed. Often the problem *involves* other people, but harming them is not the right way to solve differences. Instead, we must seek to fix the problem *together with* the other person.

The real problem is a difference in value system, and the solution to the problem requires a change in value system, either our own or another person's. Attempting to resolve anger without changing values does not solve problems; it creates more. If we inaccurately identify the source of the trouble we cannot correct it. And if we merely mask the symptom by controlling angry outbursts, we will not actually resolve the problem or the emotion.

Desires fueled by our values are the real source of conflicts and anger. Thus, anger exercised constructively evaluates one's own values. Rather than always seeking to reshape other people, we need to consider how the value of beneficial love should affect our consideration of others. Change is positive when we work together to deepen our relationships by discussing values with the hope of achieving similarity.

If there is a disagreement of values between you and me, I usually assume that you are the one who is wrong. Anytime I assume that another person and his value system is the problem to be fixed without first evaluating my own value system and seeing if the problem lies within me, I will damage my relationships. And, if I find myself often becoming angry with others, it is a symptom that there is something wrong within my own value system.

The fault is either internal or external. If it is inside

of us, we need to change our own values. If it is outside of us, then we need to fix the problem. Sometimes the problem resides in the value system of another person, and sometimes it is a difficult life experience. Either way, we must attempt to fix problems while not destroying relationships.

Of course, when a person refuses to change a conflict producing value, relationship cannot always be restored and the problem cannot always be resolved. If we suffer pain or injustice and it is impossible for us to change the value system of the one who injured us, we must allow other values to be formed within us, such as contentment or the ability to treat others better than we have been treated. If we allow the values producing anger or bitterness to control us, we also will become people who harm others.

Disgust

Although disgust is clearly a negative emotion, it is a healthy response intended to protect us. Feelings of contempt, horror, and shock are all emotions related to disgust, which is a reaction to something being out of place. When we see vomit, blood, or a broken bone sticking out of our flesh, we normally have a strong reaction to it. That reaction is our recognition that something is wrong. Stomach contents, blood, and bones do not provoke negative feelings when they remain in their natural locations.

Ethical disgust results from a person's value system being unusually different from the norm, or from society's, or from our own. The practice of certain values disgusts us because they seem so "out of place." We are shocked because someone holds such values, and that he acts on them publicly or privately. When another person's value system is offensive to us, we experience disgust, shock, and perhaps even contempt. We feel disgust because of the *great difference* between our values and the other person's.

However, when a person or group of people is constantly exposed to something disgusting, they gradually experience less disgust over it. People who work around injured or dead bodies begin to stop thinking about them in the same way. They become accustomed to what most of us find shocking.

Similarly, societal norms change when values once considered disgusting no longer produce the same effect on the majority as before. When disgust remains, there will be no change; but when there is constant exposure to the disgusting, eventually no disgust will remain. With experience or discussion, the level of disgust drops and cultural values transform. The once-rejected value becomes accepted and admitted as normal by the culture.

I once helped someone clean up a home (if one may use that word to describe such living conditions) that was wall-to-wall filth. I have never seen anything like it in my entire life! Yet the people who lived in it were not bothered by it enough to clean it up; it became normal to them. The same can happen to people morally.

In order to prevent the adoption of destructive values in our lives, there must be a sustained level of disgust for values that we reject. If we do not habitually express disgust, we will eventually be overwhelmed by the numbing effect of being bombarded with the disgusting. If we do not express disgust, others will assume that we accept the value. Without resistance to values we reject, society will collectively move toward a new norm. Afterwards we, along with our children, will be in danger of accepting it and allowing part of our own value systems to be molded after relationally destructive values.

When people embrace values that benefit only themselves, the entire society becomes selfish. It then becomes out of place to help others, rather than the custom. Beneficial love as a cultural value protects everyone from exploitation. If we want relationships to remain strong we need to promote, rather than reject, values that enhance them. A society can move from being selfishly motivated to seeking the good of others as citizens adopt beneficial love as their prime motivator.

Anger and disgust both derive from a belief that something is wrong. Disgust without anger does not have the strength to defend its value system. Anger without love seeks to resolve problems by attacking people rather than preserving relationship. The relational problems in our homes and society can be solved by promoting a value system that prompts people to act for the benefit not only of self, but also of others.

Recap:

- Anger arises from the dissonance between what life is like and what we believe it should be like.
- Anger should be used to change values and not be directed toward people.
- Disgust is a response to values that are significantly different from your own.

Think:

- How have I used anger incorrectly and how has it negatively impacted my relationships?
- Which of my values are most likely to trigger an episode of anger?

19 Fear and Hope

Fear and hope are emotions expressing personal definitions of what is "good for me" and what is "bad for me," especially related to what happens to me directly. However, do not confuse this with *moral* considerations of good and bad. Although interacting with our morals, they are not dependent on them. Although often considered religious language, the ideas behind the words "blessing" and "cursing" best express our emotions regarding fear and hope.

Thus, whatever we desire to happen to us in life is "good" or blessing; and whatever we do not wish to happen, or fear will happen to us, is "bad" or cursing. Blessing and cursing are very strong motivators, and we use them to consider the benefits and drawbacks of each of our desires. Ultimately, we define blessing as obtaining what we value and cursing as a thwarting of our values. Practically, this is the manner in which we all live.

Fear

Being cursed is the belief that harm or loss will befall what we value. Fear strikes when we believe that what we value will be taken away. The feeling of fear is negative, but fear can be useful if it moves us to prevent our fears from becoming reality. Fear is easily identified according to the three areas of desire; therefore, by examining our desires, we can learn that which we truly value.

We fear that our bodily needs will not be met, or that something will happen to us physically, including sickness, injury, and death. Fears about physical well-being reveal values of comfort and pleasure. We do not want to lose our health, mobility, or mind; nor do we want unfulfilled needs.

We fear that we will lose or not receive the power, wealth, and possessions that are important to us. Fear of losing our domain reveals the value we place on possessions and the security and safety we desire for our future. We compete with others because of what we fear we might lose, or fail to obtain or attain.

Our worry about loneliness or the loss of love reveals how much we value relationships and people. But we also fear not receiving the praise or adoration we deserve. Anxiety, shyness, embarrassment, and humiliation all reveal how much we fear people might treat us negatively and how much we value recognition.

We experience our most numerous and intense emotions in our relationships. Therefore, relationships are also the source of our greatest fears. We fear the unknown of the future, but we dread loss of relationship. Merely imagining the loss of someone we love provokes strong emotional reactions: We can fear that a relationship will experience conflict or fail; and we can fear what might happen to our children or parents regarding their safety, the outcome of their decisions, and for their relationships.

Fear causes us to hide from one another, usually because of something we value. We are afraid to reveal who we truly are because we believe it might produce conflict or embarrassment. Deeply differing values often result in relational pain that continues to produce residual fear, but striving toward similar values results in nothing to hide and the removal of fear.

Ultimately, we fear what we cannot control, and we erroneously believe that enough control can prevent us from being afraid. However, worry and fear can have a power of their own, even without a tangible loss. Fear of *potential* loss produces real emotional loss, and can be powerful enough to steal away our happiness. Our view of life, others, and happiness are all revealed in how vulnerable we feel and what, if anything, we do to alleviate our fear.

Resolving fear requires changing the values producing the anxiety. Relational fears can be removed as values are shared in the context of love and acceptance. Other fears are tied to what we have done, or to something we are afraid will be found out. We are afraid of the negative consequences, or cursing, for our actions. The four steps of resolving conflict in relationship will resolve those fears, although they may not remove the consequences we fear. That can only be done by adopting values that give us the strength to face the consequences of our selfish actions.

Selfish values produce fear because they focus on

the effect the loss will have on *self*. Values producing fear are contrary to beneficial love, so acting for the good of others resolves fears that are driven by selfish values. To experience the freedom arising from loving and helping others, we must accept loss. *Sacrifice and fear are both about loss*, but fear of loss is deadly to sacrificial living. The person who lives in fear cannot live a life of beneficial love for others.

Fears produced by what we cannot control must be dealt with by changing values that relate to accepting the issues we fear. People choose different means to accept the inevitable, but it always requires their adoption of new values that overrule the ones producing fear. Adopting a value system that embraces loss—such as sacrificial love for others—reduces fears relating to loss.

Hope

Hope is the belief that we will obtain what we value; it is the belief that we will be blessed. Hope is the cure to fear—especially runaway fear. Fear and hope both look to the future: one with optimism and one with pessimism. But hope allows us to look *beyond* fear to the future achievement of what we desire and long for.

Examining our hopes and dreams reveals our values. What do we desire and really want in terms of bodily appetites? How do we want people to respond to us? What kind of power, control, wealth, and possessions do we desire? Not everything we hope for is good for relationship; hope can also motivate us to fulfill selfish values. Thus, hope is not positive if the value system underlying it is corrupt.

Our dreams are what we want life to be like. We can

imagine what we want and how we wish to gratify our desires. We can dream of having bodily appetites fulfilled, allowing our minds to portray how we might have our cravings satisfied. We can imagine people adoring us, and we can imagine the quality of the domain we wish to possess. However, our true values are measured by what we *do* and not only by what we *dream*.

Something can be part of our value systems even though we never obtain or work toward it. For example, a person may desire wealth yet remain unwilling to strive for it. Instead he purchases lottery tickets, valuing the hope they offer. Enhancing domain is still a value for that person, but certainly not one of his strongest. Many people desire blessing in their lives, yet do little to realize it. Our hopes are shaped by our values, but they are always limited by the stronger values we possess. Ultimately, *hope is limited by how deeply we believe we can fulfill our values.*

Hope is a powerful motivator. While fear prompts us to protect ourselves, hope energizes us to achieve the values that result in our happiness. Hope enables us to live positive values because it sees the blessing at the end of sacrifice and pursues it in spite of the fear of loss.

Sacrificial love has its root in hope. Sacrificial love acknowledges loss but believes that sacrifice is not the end. We sacrifice because we hope for a better future. We hope that this world will be better because of the way we have lived. We hope that we will have made a difference to those whom we have loved.

Hope and fear are emotions that reveal our desires and values. Hope believes our values can be fulfilled and that our goals are obtainable, while fear believes they will not be fulfilled and that we will suffer loss. We must not be overwhelmed by fear; instead, we must examine the values generating it and evaluate what needs to change to free us from fear. We must also examine our hopes and dreams to make sure we are using hope's positive energy for positive purposes.

Hope in itself is not positive because we can hope for that which benefits only self, and we can be driven by hope even if our desires harm others. Striving to fulfill such dreams will ultimately bring relational destruction and loss, rather than the good we imagine. Conversely, fear itself is not always negative; it often prevents us from pursuing some of our worst values.

Do not underestimate the power of blessing and cursing. We all desire blessing and avoid cursing, and these are merely a way of expressing our heart's desires. Selfish values produce cursing in relationships, while blessings come from living the right value system. Beneficial love is a value system for those whose greatest hope revolves around building strong relationships.

Recap:

- Fear derives from the belief that we will lose something valuable to us.
- Hope overcomes our fears and empowers us to achieve our deepest values.

Think:

- How does fear limit the quality of my relationships?
- What do my greatest fears reveal is most important to me?
- How can I use hope to overcome my fears?

Learning to Love

Learning to love requires learning first about yourself and then adopting a value system to which you are truly committed. Changing from what you are to what you will become requires an honest examination of your own values and how you act in relationship. It requires skillful and willful understanding of your emotions, desires, and values.

Your emotions reveal whether or not your values are being fulfilled. Emotions are not intended to guide you in right and wrong; rather, they indicate how important each of your values is to you. The stronger your emotional reactions in life, the more important the underlying values are to you. Whenever you experience strong emotion, it is essential to consider which values are affecting you.

You express your values according to three main areas of desire: appetites, reputation, and domain. These areas of desires are not values; they are simply the outlets or means of expressing values. However, the actions you take to accomplish or prevent the fulfillment of these desires speaks volumes about the values driving them. Examine how you act or react regarding these desires.

Relationships are based on common values: if you want a relationship to grow, you must commit to growing together in value system with another person. All conflict in relationship is conflict over value system: if you want to remove conflict from a relationship, you must be willing to evaluate and change conflicting values.

Resolving conflict requires admitting fault when you are wrong, replacing the values that originated the conflict, forgiving others when they hurt you, and reconciling a relationship through agreement in values. These steps are not one-sided; it takes two people to make a relationship work. Make every effort to bring peace to your relationships by resolving conflict according to these four steps.

For relationships to be their best, they require not only common values but values that strengthen and improve relationship. The best value system for this is beneficial love (or sacrificial love for the benefit of others). With this as your core value, you possess the attitude necessary for growing closer and resolving conflict. Furthermore, your desires expressed within the confines of beneficial love will greatly enhance your relationships.

Loving others does not come automatically. It involves deliberate action in the face of differences. You can improve your relationships, and you can learn to love others more. This process begins with understanding your own values and comparing them to the relational standard of beneficial love. As you willfully change how you act toward others, your relationships can be characterized by love.